THE TASTE OF OUR TIME

Collection planned and directed by

ALBERT SKIRA

BIOGRAPHICAL AND CRITICAL STUDY

BY

GUY HABASQUE

Translated by Stuart Gilbert

Cubism

SKIRA

CHRONOLOGICAL SURVEY

The dates of birth of the painters mentioned in this book fall between 1875 and 1887, as follows:

1875 July 31, Gaston Duchamp (Jacques Villon), Damville (Eure).

1878 January 22, Francis Picabia, Paris.

1880 June 10, André Derain, Chatou (Seine-et-Oise).

1881 February 4, Fernand Léger, Argentan (Orne).
February 11, Carlo Carrà, Quargnento, Italy.
October 25, Pablo Picasso, Malaga, Spain.
December 8, Albert Gleizes, Paris.
Henri Le Fauconnier, Hesdin (Pas-de-Calais).

1882 April 29, Auguste Herbin, Quincy (Nord).
May 13, Georges Braque, Argenteuil (Seine-et-Oise).
October 19, Umberto Boccioni, Reggio di Calabria.

1883 April 7, Gino Severini, Cortona (Tuscany).
June 24, Jean Metzinger, Nantes.
November 14, Louis Markous (Marcoussis), Warsaw.

1885 April 12, Robert Delaunay, Paris.
July 5, André Lhote, Bordeaux.
July 11, Roger de La Fresnaye, Le Mans.

1887 March 23, José Victoriano Gonzalez (Juan Gris), Madrid.
July 28, Marcel Duchamp, Blainville (near Rouen).

1899 Braque is apprenticed to his father, a house-painter. Jacques Villon makes his first engravings for Edmond Sagot.

1899 Guillaume Apollinaire settles in Paris with his family.

1900 Picasso's first visit to Paris; Berthe Weill buys three sketches from him. Braque settles in Paris, renting a room in Montmartre. Léger works as an architect's draftsman in Paris.

1900 Carrà's first trip to Paris.

1901 Picasso moves from Barcelona to Madrid in February; second visit to Paris in late March; first Paris exhibition at Vollard's; strikes up a friendship with Max Jacob; beginning of his Blue Period; leaves Paris for Barcelona in late December.

1902 Picasso exhibitions at Berthe Weill's in Montmartre and at Vollard's. Third journey to Paris in October, lives with Max Jacob.

1902 Lautrec retrospectives at the Salon des Indépendants and at Durand-Ruel's.

5

1903 Picasso returns to Barcelona early in the year. Marcoussis, Metzinger and Herbin arrive in Paris. Admitted to the Ecole des Arts Décoratifs, Léger works on the side in an architect's office and as retoucher for a photographer. Villon exhibits at the Salon d'Automne. La Fresnaye enrolls at the Académie Julian. Picabia paints in the Sisley manner (1903-1908).

1903 Founding of the Salon d'Automne.

1904 Picasso returns to Paris in April and takes a studio in the Bateau-Lavoir; his Blue Period comes to an end late in the year; meets André Salmon. Herbin makes the acquaintance of Wilhelm Uhde; Clovis Sagot buys canvases from him. Villon becomes a member of the Salon d'Automne and serves on the Committee. Duchamp studies at the Académie Julian.

1904 Cézanne and Renoir rooms at the Salon d'Automne. Constantin Brancusi comes to Paris.

1905 Through Jean Mollet Picasso meets Guillaume Apollinaire, who publishes his first article on the painter in the May issue of "La Plume"; Picasso spends the summer in Holland; beginning of his Pink Period. Delaunay devotes himself entirely to painting.

1905 Seurat and Van Gogh retrospectives at the Indépendants. Manet retrospective at the Salon d'Automne. The Fauves exhibit at the Salon d'Automne.

1906 Leo and Gertrude Stein buy Picasso's "Girl with a Basket of Flowers" from Clovis Sagot; H. P. Roché introduces them to Picasso, who begins the portrait of Gertrude Stein; after 80 sittings he rubs out the face, goes off to Gosol (Spanish Pyrenees) for his holidays, and on his return finishes the portrait from memory; begins "Les Demoiselles d'Avignon" soon after and meets Matisse at the Steins'.
Braque, who has rallied to Fauvism, spends the summer at Antwerp with Friesz and autumn at L'Estaque, on the Riviera.
Gris comes to Paris, settles in the Bateau-Lavoir, and earns a living by doing cartoons for the papers.
Gleizes helps to found "L'Abbaye de Créteil" with Arcos, Mercereau and others.
After an illness, Léger spends the winter in Corsica, at Belgodère; his painting shows the influence of Impressionism.
Delaunay comes under the influence of Neo-Impressionism and becomes friendly with Metzinger, who is working on similar lines; Delaunay paints his first version of "Le Manège de cochons"; friendship with the Douanier Rousseau.

1906 Death of Cézanne at Aix-en-Provence, October 22.
Gauguin retrospective at the Salon d'Automne.
Severini and Modigliani settle in Paris.

1907 Picasso finishes "Les Demoiselles d'Avignon." Braque sells all the canvases he exhibited at the Indépendants, five to Wilhelm Uhde; spends the summer at La Ciotat, autumn at L'Estaque; Apollinaire takes him to Picasso's studio to see the "Demoiselles."
D. H. Kahnweiler settles in Paris and opens a gallery, 28 rue Vignon; exhibits Fauve pictures and contracts to buy a large part of Derain's, Braque's and Picasso's production. All three painters greatly impressed by the Cézanne retrospective at the Salon d'Automne.
Delaunay is away on military service at Laon.

1908 Picasso spends his summer holidays at La Rue-des-Bois (Oise); gives a banquet in his Paris studio in honor of the Douanier Rousseau.
Braque spends spring and summer at L'Estaque; the canvases he brings back are rejected by the jury of the Salon d'Automne; he exhibits them at Kahnweiler's (November 9-28) and Apollinaire prefaces the catalogue; reviewing the exhibition in "Gil Blas" (November 14), Louis Vauxcelles speaks of "cubes."
At the end of the year Léger moves into La Ruche, 2 Passage de Dantzig, where he lives for the next two years.
Delaunay influenced by Cézanne; meets the Russian painter Sonia Terk.
La Fresnaye enrolls at the Académie Ranson where he studies under Maurice Denis and Paul Sérusier; his work shows influences of both.
Lhote paints under the joint influence of Gauguin and Carrière.

1908 Twenty El Grecos exhibited at the Salon d'Automne.

1909 Picasso spends the summer at Horta de Ebro (Catalonia); back in Paris, he moves into a studio at 11 Boulevard de Clichy.
Braque exhibits for the last time before the war at the Indépendants and spends the summer at La Roche-Guyon (Seine-et-Oise).
Herbin moves into the Bateau-Lavoir.
Gleizes becomes friendly with Le Fauconnier and is influenced by him.
Delaunay paints his "Saint-Séverin" series.

1909 Picabia exhibits his impressionist pictures at the Georges Petit Gallery; leaves in April for Spain, memories of which inspired his abstract canvases of 1912-1914.
Kahnweiler publishes Apollinaire's "L'Enchanteur pourrissant," illustrated by Derain.

1909 First production of Diaghilev's Russian Ballet at the Châtelet theater in Paris. Marinetti's Futurist Manifesto published in the "Figaro," February 20.

1910 Picasso spends the summer at Cadaquès (Catalonia) with Fernande Olivier and Derain; makes portraits of Vollard, Uhde, Kahnweiler; both he and Braque are now gradually breaking with the single viewpoint of classical perspective (Analytical Cubism).
Marcoussis is strongly attracted by Braque's work.
Metzinger exhibits his "Portrait of Apollinaire" at the Indépendants and "Cubist Nude" at the Salon d'Automne.
Gleizes leaves the Salon de la Nationale for the Indépendants; meets Metzinger and Delaunay; influenced by Cézanne and Cubism.
Kahnweiler takes up Léger and exhibits his work.
Delaunay's "destructive" period: "Cities," "Eiffel Towers," etc. Marries Sonia Terk in November.
La Fresnaye comes under the influence of Cézanne.
Villon turns more and more from graphic work to painting.
Picabia becomes friendly with Marcel Duchamp during the winter of 1910-1911.
André Lhote exhibition at Druet's in November.
Apollinaire succeeds André Salmon as art critic on "L'Intransigeant."

1910 Rousseau exhibits "The Dream" at the Indépendants; dies on September 2.
"Comoedia" publishes the Manifesto of Futurist Painters on May 18 and "Futurist Venice" on June 17.
Mondrian and Chagall come to Paris.
In Germany: Kandinsky's first abstract paintings.
In Berlin, March 3, Herwarth Walden publishes the first number of the review "Der Sturm."

1911 Picasso spends his holidays at Céret (French Pyrenees) with Braque and the Catalan sculptor Manolo; does cubist etchings illustrating Max Jacob's "Saint Matorel," published by Kahnweiler; first one-man show in New York at the Photo-Secession Gallery (April).

1911 Juan Gris begins painting in earnest ("Portrait of Maurice Raynal"); sells his first canvases to Clovis Sagot.
Braque introduces Marcoussis to Picasso.
Apollinaire introduces Gleizes to Picasso.
Delaunay becomes friendly with Gleizes, Le Fauconnier and Apollinaire.
Villon stops working for Edmond Sagot, who is baffled by his work, and is taken up by Edmond's brother Clovis.
André Lhote comes under the influence of Cézanne.
Marcel Duchamp paints "Portrait of Chess Players" and the first version of "Nude descending a Staircase."
Cubism revealed to the public at the 27th Salon des Indépendants (Room 41). In June Léger, Delaunay, Gleizes and Le Fauconnier figure in the 8th Independent Artists' exhibition at Brussels.
Room VIII at the Salon d'Automne shocks the critics.
From November 20 to December 16, exhibition of the "Société Normande de Peinture Moderne," 3 Rue Tronchet (Metzinger, Gleizes, Le Fauconnier, Léger, Villon, Duchamp, Picabia, La Fresnaye and others).

1911 First exhibition of "Der Blaue Reiter" at Munich (December 19-early January 1912), to which Delaunay, the only living French artist invited, contributes five paintings ("Saint-Séverin," "City," "Eiffel Tower," etc.).

1912 In Paris for their first French exhibition, at Bernheim-Jeune's (February 5-24), the Futurist painters call on Picasso in his studio; in the spring he goes to Avignon and Céret, then spends the summer at Sorgues (near Avignon) with Braque; first "papiers collés"; back in Paris he moves into a new studio at 242 Boulevard Raspail. In December he signs a contract with Kahnweiler, who becomes his sole agent.
Gris exhibits three pictures at the Indépendants, including "Homage to Picasso"; in October he signs a contract with Kahnweiler, who becomes his sole agent.
Gleizes and Metzinger publish "Du Cubisme."
Delaunay spends the month of January at Laon painting views of the cathedral; exhibits in late February with Marie Laurencin at the Barbazanges Gallery; at the Indépendants exhibits his large-scale "City of Paris," highly praised by Apollinaire; Marc, Macke and Klee call on him in Paris; he takes Apollinaire in after the poet's break with Marie Laurencin; during the second half of the year his work develops along wholly new lines: "Windows," "Disk," the first "Circular Forms."
Duchamp paints the second version of "Nude descending a

Staircase"; Gleizes and Metzinger having asked him not to exhibit it alongside their works, he withdraws it the day before the Salon des Indépendants opens.

Apollinaire becomes friendly with Picabia.

Villon, Duchamp, Picabia, Gleizes and some other painters organize the "Salon de la Section d'Or" (October 10-30) where they exhibit alongside Archipenko, Gris, Marie Laurencin, Léger, Marcoussis, Metzinger, La Fresnaye, etc.; on this occasion Apollinaire and Maurice Raynal give lectures on Cubism.

After the exhibition of their works at the Salon d'Automne, a plot was hatched against the Cubists to prohibit them from exhibiting in government-owned buildings; taken up by a municipal councillor (who was also an amateur painter) named Lampué and a senator, Jules-Louis Breton, the matter was discussed in the Chamber of Deputies, where Marcel Sembat, backed by the Under-Secretary of State for Fine Arts, defended the artist's freedom of expression.

The Cubists are represented in many exhibitions abroad: Munich (Der Blaue Reiter), Cologne (Sonderbund), Berlin (Der Sturm), Zurich (Der Moderne Bund), Moscow (Jack of Diamonds), London (Grafton Galleries), Barcelona (Delmau Gallery).

1912 Beginning of Derain's "Gothic" period.

Apollinaire publishes several articles on the new painting in "Les Soirées de Paris" and writes his poem "Les Fenêtres," inspired by Delaunay's pictures.

André Salmon publishes "La Jeune Peinture française."

First "Dinner at Passy," July 6; at the fourth, December 21, homage is paid to Cézanne, eulogized by La Fresnaye.

Milan, April 11: Boccioni publishes "Technical Manifesto of Futurist Sculpture."

At Munich Kandinsky publishes "Über das Geistige in der Kunst," written in 1910, then works with Franz Marc on the articles published in book form under the title "Der Blaue Reiter."

1913 Picasso spends May and June at Céret with Gris, Braque and Max Jacob; back in Paris he moves to 5 Rue Schoelcher.

Gris remains at Céret till November; sees much of Manolo; Gertrude Stein and Léonce Rosenberg buy their first pictures by him.

On May 3 at the Académie Wassilieff Léger lectures on "The Origins of Painting and its Representative Value" (published in "Montjoie!", no. 8, May 29 and in "Der Sturm," no. 172/173, August); signs a contract in October with Kahnweiler, who becomes his sole agent.

Accompanied by Apollinaire, Delaunay goes to Berlin for his exhibition at the Der Sturm Gallery (January 27-February 20); "Der Sturm" publishes his article "Sur la lumière" translated by Klee (no. 144/145, January); friendship with Bruce, Frost and Blaise Cendrars; Sonia Delaunay and Cendrars publish the first "simultaneous book": "La Prose du Transsibérien"; first "simultaneous clothes" by Sonia Delaunay. Picabia goes to the United States; one-man show in March at Photo-Secession Gallery, New York.

Apollinaire publishes "Les Peintres cubistes" in March; becomes co-director of "Les Soirées de Paris," now owned by Serge Férat and Hélène d'Oettingen (Roch Grey); collaborates on "Montjoie!", a review launched in February by Canudo.

Revelation at the Salon des Indépendants of a new tendency towards color and abstraction: Orphism (Delaunay, Bruce, Frost, Picabia, Kupka, Russell, Macdonald-Wright).

1913 Death of Clovis Sagot in February.

First number of "Lacerba," sponsoring the Futurists, published in Florence in January; exhibition of sculpture by Boccioni at the Galerie La Boëtie, Paris (June 20-July 16); publication of Apollinaire's manifesto "The Futurist Antitradition" (June 29), then of Marc Delmarle's "Futurist Manifesto at Montmartre" (July 18), followed by polemics between the author and Severini; publication of Carrà's manifesto on "The Painting of Sounds, Noises and Smells" (August 11); Boccioni, Apollinaire and Delaunay engage in polemics on simultaneity.

Exhibition of the American "Synchromists" Morgan Russell and Stanton Macdonald-Wright at Bernheim-Jeune's (October 27-November 8).

February 17: opening of the International Exhibition of Modern Art (Armory Show) in New York, at which all avant-garde tendencies are represented for the first time in America; Duchamp's "Nude descending a Staircase" scandalizes the public; the exhibition later moves on to Boston and Chicago.

Berlin: first "Herbstsalon" organized by "Der Sturm," with many French painters represented (September 20-November 1).

May 29: first performance of Stravinsky's "Rite of Spring" at the Théâtre des Champs-Elysées, Paris.

1914 Picasso illustrates Max Jacob's "Le Siège de Jérusalem," published by Kahnweiler; leaves in June for Tarascon and Avignon, where he joins Braque and Derain.

Gris leaves in June for Collioure, where Matisse and Marquet are working.

Herbin exhibition at the Galerie Moderne in March.

Gleizes, Metzinger, Duchamp-Villon and Villon exhibit together in Paris at the Galerie Groult in April, at the Der Sturm Gallery in Berlin in June.

La Fresnaye exhibits at the Levesque Gallery in April, Metzinger at the Weill Gallery and Lhote at the Vildrac Gallery in May.

On May 9 Léger lectures at the Académie Wassilieff on "Pictorial Achievements Today" (published by "Les Soirées de Paris," no. 25, June 15).

August 2: outbreak of the First World War. Braque, Metzinger, Gleizes, Léger and Villon are called up; Marcoussis, La Fresnaye, Kupka and Apollinaire volunteer.

1914 March 2: sale at the Hôtel Drouot of the collection of modern painting known as "La Peau de l'Ours," founded in 1904 by André Level.

Arthur Cravan's review of the Salon des Indépendants in "Maintenant" starts off a violent controversy with Delaunay and Apollinaire.

May 21: Rimsky-Korsakov's "Coq d'Or" performed at the Paris Opera with sets by Nathalie Gontcharova.

Larionov and Nathalie Gontcharova exhibit "rayonist" paintings at Paul Guillaume's (June 18-30).

Apollinaire publishes his first "Calligrammes."

July: Mondrian goes back to Holland.

THE BEGINNINGS OF CUBISM

Few can have guessed at the time it was made that the picture which Pablo Picasso worked on in the winter of 1906-1907, and which now is known as *Les Demoiselles d'Avignon*, was destined to have so decisive an effect on all modern painting.

Born at Malaga in 1881, the young Spanish artist had then been living for two and a half years in a rather squalid studio, formerly occupied by his compatriot the sculptor Paco Durio, in the Rue Ravignan on the slope of the Butte Montmartre. He had already made a name for himself among the younger generation of artists at Barcelona, where he had lived from 1895 to 1904, but his reputation had not crossed the frontier and he had a struggle to make ends meet during those early years in Paris. This is reflected in the works of the Blue Period and even those of his Pink Period, up to 1906, the year in which he ceased painting emaciated beggars, cripples and tragic-eyed circus folk and took to less sentimental, more constructive methods of expression. Thus the *Portrait of Gertrude Stein* (Metropolitan Museum, New York)—Miss Stein had just discovered his talent and struck up a friendship with the young artist—like the *Self-Portrait* (Gallatin Collection, Philadelphia Museum of Art) made in 1906, showed that he now was less concerned with bringing out the personalities of his models than with simplifying forms and generalizing volumes.

It was shortly after making these portraits that Picasso embarked on that huge composition (nearly eight feet square) *Les Demoiselles d'Avignon*, which consists of a group of five female nudes, the only ornamental element being a little heap of fruit in the foreground. In the first version the bodies were painted flat, almost without modeling, with darker or lighter lines so placed as to suggest their essential forms, but without individualizing them. The first persons allowed to inspect the picture remarked that the bodies looked as if they had been "hacked out with an ax." Influences of Catalan Romanesque painting are clearly visible in the rendering of the young women's features, reduced to a schematic pattern: the eyes composed of one or two oval contour lines enclosing black, expressionless pupils, a single Z-shaped line linking the eyebrow with the nose shown in profile, and a thin line for the mouth. There is no impression of volume in any of the figures.

It was the problem of volumes that was to preoccupy the artist during the second half of that winter of 1906-1907. Putting aside his big canvas for the time being, he tried to solve it in a number of studies, mostly figures, but also a few still lifes. Some vividly colored, others in near-monochrome, these studies served as stepping-stones towards the final solution. Here Picasso's aim was to suggest volume without recourse to chiaroscuro and the question was: how to make relief perceptible on a flat surface without demarcating zones of light and shade which seem to "hollow out" the canvas? This problem became particularly acute when the artist had to represent projecting volumes such as the nose which, seen from in front, forms a perpendicular spanning the facial plane. Picasso ended up by flattening it against the cheek so as to avoid any effect of perspective, and by replacing zones of shadow with long, parallel lines of color. This was the technique he opted for in *Les Demoiselles d'Avignon*, though we find it employed only in the two figures on the right, the picture being left unfinished.

All the regular visitors to Picasso's studio, his friends and neighbors, were bewildered by this strange new technique. Few grasped the importance of the problem he had solved, he was the butt of ridicule, and even the young poets who were watching his experiments with fascinated interest—Max Jacob, André Salmon and Guillaume Apollinaire—admitted they could not make head or tail of *Les Demoiselles*. Some invited friends

to come and see this "highly peculiar" picture, with a view to observing their reactions. Thus one day Apollinaire brought to the studio the young Fauve painter, Georges Braque. He, too, was dumbfounded by what he saw and embarked on a long discussion with Picasso. "You may give all the explanations you like," he is reported to have said, "but your painting makes one feel as if you were trying to make us eat cotton waste and wash it down with kerosene."

Yet Braque was evidently impressed by the young Spaniard's singular achievement, for influences of *Les Demoiselles d'Avignon* are plain to see in his large *Nude*, painted in the winter of 1907-1908. Not only are forms simplified in this picture and volumes stressed, but the volumes are demarcated with heavy outlines and modeling is indicated in most cases by broad parallel brush-strokes. Meanwhile, however, the ex-Fauve proceeded to subdue his colors, reducing his palette to a gamut of reddish-browns and ochres broken only by some discreet touches of blue and grey. Thus his evolution took an opposite course to that of Picasso, whose earlier works (notably those of the Blue and Pink Periods) had been more in the nature of lightly tinted monochromes, and who did not apply himself to investigating problems of color until 1907. Whether the fact that Fauvism was so much "in the air" at the time played any part in the change that now came over his art must remain an open question; it would be rash to make any definite pronouncement on this point. There can, however, be no doubt that if Picasso owed anything to the Fauve movement, his debt was limited to the use of pure colors in a small number of his works; for the hedonism of Fauve esthetic was basically foreign to his own, austerer temperament.

On the other hand, much has been said of the influence of Negro statuary on this phase of Picasso's evolution; some art historians, indeed, have called it his "Negro Period." Picasso has on several occasions denied that he learnt anything from African carvings and (with good reason, in our opinion) pointed out that if any influence is to be found in his work of this period it is that of medieval Spanish art. He is even reported to have said: "Negro art? Never heard of it!" Obviously the remark was not meant to be taken literally; all he wanted to convey was that he had never drawn inspiration from African sculpture —for he certainly had heard about it from his friends the Fauves, who were in fact the "discoverers" of Negro art. Kees van Dongen had a studio in the same building as himself and there he often met the two Chatou painters, Maurice Vlaminck and André Derain. Van Dongen left Montmartre in 1906, but in the previous year Derain had settled into a studio in the Rue Tourlaque on the "sacred hill" and Picasso and he soon became great friends. Finally, some months before making Braque's acquaintance, Picasso, who had just completed his portrait of Gertrude Stein, met Henri Matisse in the studio she shared with her brother Leo, which was then the favorite rendez-vous of a number of avant-garde painters. Thus, though never actually a member of the Fauve group, Picasso had fairly frequent contacts with it and when, around 1905, the Fauves "discovered" African sculpture, he was not the last of the younger men to develop an interest in it.

We shall probably never know who first had the idea of buying one of those Negro statuettes which had until then been regarded as mere curios, hardly works of art at all. Some chroniclers of the period say it was Matisse, but Vlaminck has always stoutly maintained that the credit should go to him alone. One thing is certain; the young artists of the time were all enthusiasm for Negro art and took to collecting, so far as their means permitted, masks and statuettes of greatly varying origins and—it must be admitted—of very unequal merit. For ethnological considerations weighed little with them and what so much delighted them was the way in which these Negro craftsmen had succeeded in recreating nature without copying it; and in particular their knack of representing the human face and body by methods that, while utterly unlike those of the traditional sculpture of the West, were, plastically, no less valid.

PABLO PICASSO (1881). HEAD, WINTER 1906-1907.
PRIVATE COLLECTION, PARIS.

PABLO PICASSO (1881). HEAD, WINTER 1906-1907.
PRIVATE COLLECTION, PARIS.

This revelation of Negro art fully justified the line of research Picasso was then pursuing. Indeed the view that he got from it the solution of the problem that was obsessing him at this stage of his career would carry conviction—were it not that an objective study of his work belies it. True, there are obvious similarities between certain Negro masks and some of Picasso's studies for *Les Demoiselles d'Avignon,* but a close examination of the technical means employed in the two cases rules out the likelihood of any direct influence. Since there can be no question that the problem Picasso set himself and solved was that of a new method of rendering volumes on a *flat* surface, it is hard to see how those sculptures could have really been of help. Moreover, the same problem had already been tackled by Cézanne, notably in the works of his last ten years.

By faithfully recording the color sensations apprehended by the retina the Impressionists had dealt a rude blow to the traditional vision of nature. One of the notable discoveries of this new way of seeing—with a virgin eye—was that shadows are not black. By painting objects exactly as they saw them, and not as they had been trained to paint in art schools such as Gleyre's, they had got rid of the prevailing dinginess of most academic painting and given the utmost brilliance to color. But in fighting the cause of color, they often tended—this is anyhow true of Monet, Pissarro, Sisley, and even Renoir—to exalt it at the expense of form and volume. Cézanne was alone in clearly seeing there were two sides to the question. While, loyal to the spirit of his generation, he made good his faith in color, he nonetheless refused to break faith with form and was deeply, indeed agonizingly, conscious of the need for somehow reconciling these two aspects of reality, which visual experience seems to pit against each other.

As an Impressionist, Cézanne interpreted form and color simultaneously by means of small, independent brushstrokes.

PABLO PICASSO (1881). LES DEMOISELLES D'AVIGNON (DETAIL), 1906-1907.
MUSEUM OF MODERN ART, NEW YORK.

◀ Picasso painted many preliminary studies before arriving at a solution of the spatial problem set by *Les Demoiselles d'Avignon*; it seems, however, that the notion of folding over the plane of the nose upon the face struck him only when he was making a small plaster model of the same subject. This was not the only time he resorted to a countercheck of this type. The successive stages of this formal evolution can be followed to perfection in the three figures here reproduced.

"Line and color," he told Emile Bernard, "are inseparable. In the act of painting you are drawing, and the better the colors harmonize, the more accurate is the drawing. When color is at its richest, form is at its fullest." But his stroke was very different from the impressionist comma-like touches; these colored, whereas all Cézanne's strokes constructed. Emile Bernard rightly observed that, despite his keen desire to follow nature, Cézanne "always interpreted, never copied what he saw. The seat of his vision was far more in his brain than in his eye." This is why his works, especially the last ones, have a solidity that strongly contrasts with the shimmering haze of forms we find in most impressionist pictures.

When in October 1907, the great Cézanne Memorial Exhibition took place at the Salon d'Automne, it was nothing short of a revelation to the younger painters, who for the most part knew little or nothing of his work. Not that he had been forgotten when he went into voluntary exile at Aix; it was simply that the new men were too young to have profited by his two last exhibitions in Paris. Painters of Braque's and Picasso's generation were mere boys when the large-scale exhibition of his work was held at Vollard's gallery in 1895, and even in 1904 when a whole room at the Salon d'Automne was devoted to Cézanne, none of them had really got beyond the 'prentice stage —even if that stage, as in Picasso's case, was one of brilliant promise. They were too inexperienced to understand the deeper implications of Cézanne's esthetic. By 1907, however, Picasso's intensive research work during the previous winter had to some extent prepared the ground, and the lessons of the Memorial Exhibition were not lost on them.

To evaluate the exact importance of any specific influence in the birth of an art movement is always a delicate problem. This much is sure: that the works produced by Picasso in 1907 set forth the premises of the new pictorial language and that

GEORGES BRAQUE (1882). NUDE, WINTER 1907-1908.
PRIVATE COLLECTION, PARIS.

Les Demoiselles d'Avignon may be regarded as the first cubist painting. Thus Cézanne's influence seems to have borne less on the actual data of the problem now confronted by Picasso than on the practical methods needed for its solution.

For though he was still primarily concerned with representing volume on a two-dimensional surface, Picasso's 1908 technique was very different from that of the previous year. After ruling out chiaroscuro, he now reverted to it and, what is more, gave it extreme prominence. Vivid colors are replaced by a limited range of subdued tones: greys, ochres, browns, dark red and green. Losing its freedom and fluency, the drawing is confined to rendering the exact outlines of objects reduced to their minimal terms. As a result volumes acquire a quite remarkable, almost sculpturesque relief. For the still lifes he painted at this time—for example *Bowls and Jug* (Gallatin Collection, Philadelphia Museum)—Picasso deliberately chose objects with very simple forms: bowls, jars, bottles, flasks, vases, fruit and so forth. And from La Rue-des-Bois (Oise), where he spent his summer holiday in 1908, he brought back some monochrome landscapes in which trees and houses are likewise reduced to their essential elements.

Meanwhile, at L'Estaque, Georges Braque was passing through a very similar phase. It was at this small village near Marseilles that in the autumn of 1906 he had had his first experience of the dazzling light of Southern France and joined the ranks of the Fauves. But now, in 1908, he failed to regain that first fine rapture; the glamorous colors of the South had lost their fascination, and what he now sought to capture was the solid and enduring substance behind forms. Following on the self-questionings induced by *Les Demoiselles d'Avignon*, Cézanne's lesson had borne fruit and in this out-of-the-way village, where Cézanne himself had so often worked, Braque painted landscapes in which his aim was no longer to reproduce

PABLO PICASSO (1881). LA RUE-DES-BOIS, 1908.
PRIVATE COLLECTION, PARIS.

GEORGES BRAQUE (1882). ROAD NEAR L'ESTAQUE, 1908.
MUSEUM OF MODERN ART, NEW YORK.

PABLO PICASSO (1881). BOWLS AND JUG, 1908.
PHILADELPHIA MUSEUM OF ART, GALLATIN COLLECTION.

more or less transient color impressions, but to body forth collectively the most stable elements of the scene. In these landscapes treetrunks are recorded in the shape of cylinders, leafage has a new solidity and windowless houses, betraying nothing of the life within, have become as much a part of nature as the nearby rocks. Here Braque restricts his palette to ochres and

GEORGES BRAQUE (1882). GUITAR AND ACCORDION, 1908.
OWNED BY THE ARTIST.

various shades of green with some touches of brown and bluish-grey, while a rudimentary chiaroscuro gives relief to the projecting edges of volumes. Allowing for differences of style and temperament, Braque's technique was much the same as Picasso's.

Daniel-Henry Kahnweiler has described these works as "the first serious attempt to follow the path Cézanne had opened up." And in fact this phase of Cubism may be described as Cézannesque in several respects; notably in the artist's evident purpose of restoring to objects that density and substantiality of which they had been drained little by little by an over-exclusive preoccupation with effects of light.

What Picasso and Braque were aiming at was to get back to the *durable* form of the thing seen, by eliminating incidentals, bringing out as clearly as possible prototypal geometric forms —more or less regular polyhedra, cylinders and cones—and "paneling" planes with them. Mention is often made of a passage in a letter dated April 15, 1904, from Cézanne to Emile Bernard (published, as it so happened, in 1907). "Nature should be treated in terms of the cylinder, the sphere, the cone, and all laid out in perspective, i.e. so that each side of an object or a plane converges on a central point." But we run a risk of garbling Cézanne's real meaning if this remark is arbitrarily isolated from its context and an inference be drawn that he was in any sense the "creator" of Cubism. For it is far from certain that, had he lived as long as, say, Degas or Monet, he would have wholeheartedly approved of what the Cubists were doing. Indeed we may surmise that he would have found some exaggeration (to say the least) in the way these young men stressed form at the expense of light and color. In the same letter he goes on to say: "Nature as the human eye perceives it is more in depth than on the surface; hence the need for introducing into our light vibrations, rendered by reds and yellows, a suitable quantity of bluish tints so as to give the

GEORGES BRAQUE (1882). STILL LIFE, 1909.
HERMANN RUPF COLLECTION, BERN.

sense of air." And air was, in fact, conspicuously absent from Picasso's and Braque's compositions. Cézanne had often raised the horizon line, but they raised it even more drastically, with the result that only a deliberately limited tract of open space remained; the rendering of atmosphere was reduced to a minimum, and the picture space filled with objects echeloned against a background brought as close as possible.

In this respect the structure of their landscapes is significant. Houses, trees and rocks are systematically used to mask the horizon line, so as to avoid suggestions of a limitless expanse of sky and the need for rendering light effects. Lighting is reduced to a chiaroscuro that is more ideal than realistic and models volumes without taking account of variations of intensity in the source of light and its play on objects. Color, sparingly applied, is sacrificed to the expression of volumes. Theoretically both Picasso and Braque aimed at rendering solely the local colors of each object—that is to say, its "real" color, independently of the changes caused by light—though they had perforce to accept those variations of intensity in zones of shadow which are basic to chiaroscuro.

It is therefore a mistake to assume that Cézanne's influence, considerable though it was, exercised an unqualified ascendancy and that, as some would have us believe, all Cubism was implicit in the works of the Aix master's final period. Not that this is in any way to be regretted; what is needed for an influence to be truly fruitful is not blind submission on the part of those who undergo it—rather, a discriminating choice of such elements as are most authentically new. In Cézanne's works we find passages still purely impressionist in inspiration, combined with architectonic, spatial values of a wholly original order. And by discarding the former and concentrating on the latter Picasso and Braque turned to account those elements of his art which were most susceptible of development.

The necessity of making such a choice becomes evident when we compare their works with those that André Derain was producing at this time. Derain, too, had been much impressed by the Cézanne Memorial Exhibition and had realized that a more rigorous, architecturally ordered composition now was needed. Abandoning the intensive use of pure colors—"That's a job for dyers," he informed Vlaminck, much to the latter's consternation—he, too, began to concentrate on volumes and to subordinate the various pictorial elements to the overall structure of the picture. But, unlike the Cubists, he kept scrupulously to Cézanne's program. Like him he held that "line and color are inseparable" and refused to sacrifice, even as a temporary expedient, one to the other. Moreover, faithful to tradition, he regarded atmosphere as the natural means of binding the picture elements together and accordingly persisted in enveloping them with light. This reluctance to depart from the rules established by his predecessors was doubtless due to an imperfectly assimilated classical culture and, in the event, had disastrous effects on his art.

Unable to free himself from the thrall of a too greatly venerated master, Derain failed to advance beyond the point reached by Cézanne. At the time he gave a misleading impression; for though they did not include him among the Cubists, his friends and admirers believed he was about to follow a parallel path. His stay with Picasso at Cadaquès in 1910 lent color to this view. During that year, carried away by the fervor of his friend's convictions, Derain produced the most "advanced" canvases of his career. But the rise of Analytical Cubism was to put an end to this equivocal situation. For Derain was at heart a classicist, deeply imbued with the traditions of the masters whom he had so closely studied in the Louvre, and he was dismayed by the revolutionary aspect of this new phase of Cubism. Instead of following the bold line of evolution traced out by his friends, he wound up by adopting a neo-classicism, tentative to start with but becoming more and more reactionary as time went on.

With Picasso and Braque, on the other hand, the Cézannesque phase was short-lived. Though at first sight the works they produced during the first months of 1909 might seem to differ little from those of the previous year, they contained new

PABLO PICASSO (1881). LANDSCAPE AT HORTA DE EBRO, 1909.
PRIVATE COLLECTION, PARIS.

GEORGES BRAQUE (1882). LA ROCHE-GUYON, 1909.
PRIVATE COLLECTION, ROUBAIX.

elements, rich in promise for the future, that soon led to a total revision of their original technique. True, the landscapes painted by Picasso at Horta de Ebro, a Catalan village near Tarragona where he spent the summer, recall those he painted at La Rue-des-Bois, just as Braque's La Roche-Guyon landscapes remind us of those he painted at L'Estaque, owing to their more or less "cubic" volumes and an insistent use of chiaroscuro. Nevertheless the later works no longer have that compact, compulsive modeling which gave the early ones an all-over uniform density and weight. Volumes now are fretted and indented by what have since been called "passages": that is to say, slight breaks in their outlines. Instances of this can be found in some of Cézanne's works but these were due, in his case, to the difficulties of achieving a structural concordance between linear representation and representation in terms of color—those "points of contact" as he called them, which were one of the master's obsessions. Picasso and Braque used "passages" with a somewhat different object: that of alleviating the monotony of over-continuous effects of light and shade along the salient edges of volumes.

It was for the same reason that in the latter half of 1909 Picasso took to breaking up large volumes into series of smaller ones, with the result that he was free to organize and direct the play of light on the objects represented as he thought best. His handling of such a work as *Woman with Pears* (Samuel A. Marx Collection, Chicago) is significant in this respect. Particularly noteworthy is the protuberance he imposes on his model's forehead so as to avoid having to graduate light evenly over a large uniform surface. In some more advanced, probably slightly later works, such as *Seated Woman* (Georges Salles Collection, Paris) or *Young Female Nude* (Museum of Modern Western Art, Moscow), both of which date to the end of 1909, he combined "passages" with the fragmentation described above

PABLO PICASSO (1881). WOMAN WITH PEARS, 1909.
MR AND MRS SAMUEL A. MARX, CHICAGO.

and thus gave his line a much greater independence than its previous function—that of circumscribing volumes—had hitherto permitted.

We now find the artists' preoccupation with volumes gradually giving place to one with planes. Surprising though it may seem at first sight, this shift of interest was natural enough and should not be taken to mean that the young Cubists were unsure of their intentions. In strict logic it could no doubt be alleged that in acting thus they were going back on their original program, that of restoring to volume its weight and density; actually, however, this seeming contradiction did not strike so deep as one might think. For though the new direction given their art told, undeniably, against the primacy of volume, it respected the truth of the object and at the same time enabled them considerably to limit the use of chiaroscuro—which in any case had been regarded as a mere temporary makeshift. Volume had served as a stalking-horse in the earliest phase of Cubism because it seemed, at the time, the only means of countering the general haziness and fugitive effects of Impressionism. Once a more efficacious method of attaining this end had been discovered, there was no longer any good reason for the young artists to cling to a procedure whose major element had, in fact, always irked them.

In any case the transition from one technique to another was effected on purely experimental lines, by tentative approximations, so that it is impossible to draw any exact chronological dividing line between the two. Some works dating to the beginning of 1910—for example, *Girl with a Mandolin* (versions in Museum of Modern Western Art, Moscow, and Roland Penrose Collection, London)—still show a preoccupation with volumes, whereas the portraits of Vollard and Wilhelm Uhde, painted in the same period, already point the way to Analytical Cubism. The most that can be said is that Picasso's evolution seems to have proceeded more rapidly than Braque's. Calmer by nature than his Spanish friend, Braque was more intent on consolidating his discoveries than with making new ones. Thus he maintained the appearances of volume over a longer period, as can be seen in *Piano and Mandola*, dating to the middle of the winter 1909-1910 (Solomon R. Guggenheim Museum, New York). We get an impression that in so doing Braque was playing for safety, that is to say endeavoring to spare the unprepared spectator the shocks and bewilderment occasioned by some of Picasso's canvases.

For the public, still in two minds about the Impressionists, might well see in these pictures, with their dovetailed and overlapping planes, no more than an aggregate of geometric forms signifying nothing. Braque had had a painful experience of what such lack of comprehension led to. On his return from L'Estaque in 1908 he had submitted six of his recent pictures to the selection committee of the Salon d'Automne and, despite the fact that the committee included the work of several friends of his—among them Matisse, Marquet and Rouault—they had rejected them all. And though Marquet contrived to get a "second chance" for one of his pictures, Braque, deeply incensed, withdrew it. Finally he decided to exhibit his new works in a small gallery that had just been opened in the Rue Vignon by a young German picture dealer, Daniel-Henry Kahnweiler.

This exhibition (November 9-28, 1908) comprised some thirty pictures, most of them painted in the previous summer at L'Estaque, and the catalogue was prefaced by the poet Guillaume Apollinaire, then making his début as art critic. The preface contained a violent attack on Impressionism, "that maelstrom of diverse, more or less noble temperaments, feverishly, impetuously, irrationally trying to express their sense of wonder at the sight of Nature"; also a glowing encomium of Braque's efforts to give art a new direction.

Though little notice of the exhibition was taken by professional critics, one article can claim a place in the *petite histoire* of art, since in it the word "cubes" was used for the first time, thus giving rise to the name which was to cover the whole movement. We have in mind the article in *Gil Blas* of November 14, 1908, in which Louis Vauxcelles wrote: "M. Braque is a very daring young man. He has been emboldened by the puzzling experiments of Picasso and Derain. Also, perhaps, obsessed unduly by Cézanne's style and memories of the static art of the Egyptians. He constructs metallic, distorted, outrageously simplified figures. He despises form and reduces everything—houses, landscapes, figures—to geometrical designs, to cubes. But we must not make fun of him, he is certainly sincere. So let's wait and see." The reference to "cubes" was, it seems, suggested to Vauxcelles by a remark of Matisse who, speaking of the canvases submitted by Braque to the Salon d'Automne, had drawn attention to the drawing and said that the rejected pictures were made of "little cubes." The adjectives "cubic" and "cubist," then the noun "cubism," made their appearance in the press during the following year. As a matter of fact, however, 1909 and 1910 were relatively calm years so far as publicity was concerned; neither critics nor public attached any great importance to the new art movements.

One of the reasons was that neither Picasso nor Braque was out to create a sensation or even to catch the public eye. The former never exhibited in the Salons, and the latter, after sending in another two canvases to the Salon des Indépendants in 1909, followed his example. Well aware that the work they were now producing was so novel that it could only provoke the derision or resentment of the masses, they saw no point in furnishing matter for idle or malicious talk. The discerning few who took a serious interest in their venture went to see their latest works in their studios or at Kahnweiler's gallery.

As early as the winter of 1907-1908 Kahnweiler, much impressed by the new painting, had taken to exhibiting Picasso, and shortly afterwards he rendered the same service to Derain and Braque, while reserving to himself the right of handling their entire output. Though the public at large knew little of his small gallery—Kahnweiler had given up one-man shows after the Braque exhibition—it was patronized by a small, select group of art lovers and collectors. This included Leo and Gertrude Stein (whose enthusiasm for Picasso had steadily increased since their first meeting), the French collector Roger Dutilleul, the Swiss Hermann Rupf, the German Wilhelm Uhde and the Russian Sergei Shchukin whose collections now bulk large in the Museum of Modern Western Art at Moscow. Thanks to their patronage the young picture dealer was able to pay "his" painters a regular allowance and, though his protégés were not yet on the road to fortune, they were anyhow spared the extreme poverty of the recent past.

This aid was all the more welcome to Picasso since Vollard, who had bought many of his pictures in the years 1906-1907, was showing less and less appreciation of the new phase of his art. Now that he no longer had to live from hand to mouth, Picasso on his return from Horta de Ebro in 1909, rented an apartment in the Boulevard de Clichy where he could work under better conditions. Still it was not without a pang of regret that he quitted the ramshackle nest of studios on the Rue Ravignan nicknamed the Bateau-Lavoir (on the strength of its resemblance to a Seine laundry-barge), scene of so many memories of his youth and the birthplace of Cubism.

PABLO PICASSO (1881). SEATED WOMAN, LATE 1909.
GEORGES SALLES COLLECTION, PARIS.

ANALYTICAL CUBISM

THE value of the chronological divisions made by art historians is always somewhat arbitrary. Nonetheless they are helpful, often indispensable, for an understanding of the general development of a movement, and of the factors determining its successive phases. The division of Cubism into precisely dated periods is a task all the more delicate since (as already noted) the painters moved forward circumspectly, sometimes halting on the way, and even, on occasion, harking back to earlier methods. All the same, most historians agree in regarding 1910 as a cardinal year, marking the end of the first phase and the beginning of a new period, in which, despite continuous experimentation and a variety of trends, we discern a certain stabilization of the artists' intellectual approach and a more or less continuous, if tentative, use of certain forms and technical procedures. Later, Juan Gris gave this second period the name of Analytical Cubism: the name under which it is still known.

For it was in 1910 that Picasso and Braque broke for good with the classical way of seeing which had obtained for over four centuries. Abolishing the single viewpoint of Albertian perspective, they now viewed the object from a multiplicity of angles and thus achieved a new, completer, more rationalized vision. Needless to say, this innovation was not due, as some art historians think or profess to think, to a sudden illumination or to the application of some mathematical theory; it was a logical consequence of the experiments they had been making in the previous year. It was the increasing importance of the part assigned to planes, as a result of the breaking up of volumes, that gave the two painters the idea of completely liberating volumes from perspective. Already, in the most advanced works produced in 1909, such as Picasso's *Seated Woman* (Georges

Salles Collection, Paris) and some of Braque's still lifes, they had been led to straighten up certain planes or tilt them slightly so as to counteract effects of lighting, and it was this procedure that Picasso resumed and generalized in the summer of 1910.

Thus in the *Portrait of Daniel Henry Kahnweiler* what immediately strikes us is the way in which planes are detached from volumes so as to present them in front view. The solid volume of the head, for example, still exists by implication, though it is no longer visible, since the planes of which it is composed have been abstracted and moved forward to the picture surface. True, they are dovetailed and superimposed in a manner still consistent with visual logic, but there is no real use of shading for locating them in space. It is now the alternation of bright and dark planes which by creating an interplay of luminous values assigns to them their relative positions. And while there is no question that this arrangement of lights and darks still owes something to the traditional principles of aerial perspective, chiaroscuro has ceased to play its classical part as a means of modeling forms.

It is not to be denied that this dissociation of planes gives such works a somewhat "hermetic" aspect and, while bringing out the intrinsic beauty of the purely plastic elements, sometimes detracts from the legibility of the picture as a whole. Hence a diminution of their representative quality or, since the term "representative" is in disfavor nowadays, what might better be styled (if at the risk of seeming pedantic) their "cognitive" quality. Some of Picasso's canvases, notably those dating from his holidays at Cadaqués, and some of the still lifes Braque painted in the winter of 1910-1911, are of such a nature that we are unable mentally to reconstitute the objects they purport to depict. In particular it is not always easy to distinguish between the outlines of objects and those that demarcate the boundaries of planes. Applied to the canvas in small,

PABLO PICASSO (1881). PORTRAIT OF D. H. KAHNWEILER, 1910.
COLLECTION MRS GILBERT CHAPMAN, GIFT TO THE ART INSTITUTE OF CHICAGO.

dappled touches or in light scumbles, colors are rendered in gradations of grey and ochre which, while giving the picture an exceptional luminosity, no longer convey the natural color of the objects represented.

This hermetic quality grew less pronounced as the two painters gradually mastered their technique. For to begin with they kept fairly close to the traditional way of seeing and one gets the impression that the planes disposed upon the picture surface have floated up, so to speak, from some three-dimensional object of a "classical" order, whose unseen presence we sense behind the screen formed by the canvas. In the last analysis, this impression, which we still have in, for example, Picasso's superb *Female Nude* (Arensberg Collection, Philadelphia Museum) and in many of Braque's works dating to 1910 and even the beginning of 1911, derives from the fact that the formal elements are still abstracted from a model, whether actually posed, as in the *Portrait of Kahnweiler*, or an imagined presence. But once the artists felt sure enough of themselves to dispense with models and to use personal, purely conceptual images as their point of departure, their works ceased to produce this impression, since instead of assembling planes detached from their natural setting, they now took to representing certain significant aspects of the object, thus facilitating its recognition. Not that the planes went out of use; only they tied up with the forms actually existing on the canvas, not with those of a model hypothetically present in the background.

This difference can be best explained by reference to a concrete example. In the above-mentioned *Female Nude* it is clear that the planes in the lower portion of the composition issue from a woman's body, since the head retains a figurative appearance, but this figurative element is omitted in other pictures. Moreover, even in the case of the *Female Nude*, if we cover up the head so that only the planes of the body are

PABLO PICASSO (1881). FEMALE NUDE, WINTER 1910-1911.
PHILADELPHIA MUSEUM OF ART, ARENSBERG COLLECTION.

visible, it is almost impossible to tell what they represent. On the other hand, in such a work as Picasso's *Still Life with "Le Journal"* we have no trouble in relating the various planes to the glass and the newspaper on the table, for the good reason that, some of the outlines of these objects being clearly stated, this relation makes itself felt, instinctively.

GEORGES BRAQUE (1882). THE FLUTE, 1910.
PHILADELPHIA MUSEUM OF ART, GALLATIN COLLECTION.

GEORGES BRAQUE (1882). THE CANDLESTICK, 1910.
HERMANN RUPF COLLECTION, BERN.

PABLO PICASSO (1881). THE POET, 1911.
PEGGY GUGGENHEIM COLLECTION, VENICE.

This is because the artist no longer aims (as he did to begin with) at abstracting the formal qualities of a subject, but at recording on his canvas a group of simultaneous aspects particularly representative of the object in question. Thus a bottle may be represented as seen both vertically and in cross-section, horizontally, so as to convey both its profile and its roundness. It is only after the model was dispensed with—towards the end of 1910—that we can speak of a definitive break with classical perspective. For in such works as the *Portrait of Kahnweiler* the use of multiple viewpoints had affected planes alone; and the subject *as a whole* was observed and rendered in terms of monocular vision. The relative slowness of the change-over and the way in which it was effected make it clear that this break was not the result of any predetermined theory, but empirical: a consequence of daily experimentation, brush in hand.

Nor was there anything theoretical about the manner in which Picasso and Braque multiplied viewpoints, and it is a great mistake to talk, as some have done, of "descriptive geometry." Surely a glance at the illustrations in this volume is enough to prove that the object is not in any sense "described" (as so many writers on the subject have declared) by its ground-plan and elevation. Quite often, indeed, a simple, single aspect suffices to express it. This is the case with the fans that figure in many of Picasso's still lifes of the 1910-1912 period, for instance *L'Indépendant* (Harry Clifford Collection). Also with a great many details or fragments of objects, such as the sound-holes and pegs of violins, drawer-knobs, nails, etc., so often found in the works of 1911 and 1912. Besides the fact that the mere multiplication of angles of vision would not necessarily provide any supplementary indications of their subjects, the two painters, well aware that some of their canvases were hard to decipher, counted on the legibility of such elements as these to make them relatively understandable.

PABLO PICASSO (1881). L'INDÉPENDANT, 1911.
COLLECTION OF HARRY CLIFFORD.

PABLO PICASSO (1881). STILL LIFE WITH "LE JOURNAL", 1912.
PRIVATE COLLECTION, PARIS.

The common notion that Picasso and Braque made a practice of "walking around the object" and then recording its successive aspects, is likewise erroneous. Their real purpose was not to present a sequence of haphazard views of the same object, but to exhibit those of its aspects which characterized its form most clearly and best revealed its fundamental nature. Moreover these various aspects were very seldom displayed separately; usually they were fused into a single, more or less coherent image. This is something quite other than the juxtaposition of various aspects of the same object viewed from different, conflicting angles, that we sometimes find in photographic montages. Such a technique would have meant only a partial deviation from classical perspective—a fragmentation, not a total rejection of its conventions. What Picasso and Braque were aiming at was a completely new mode of presentation, based on a more conceptual apprehension of the object.

A system of this kind inevitably led to drastic changes in the treatment of space. For it was not merely the principle of the convergence of lines leading to a vanishing point, and the use of a single source of illumination, that were being abandoned, but also certain canons that had prevailed for centuries, such as that of the opacity of solid bodies and the concordance of form and color. Henceforth the object, rendered by purely linear means, lost density and consistence—almost, one might say, substantiality. Doubtless volume still existed in the potential state, since, for example, the outlines of a glass continued to express its cylindrical form, but it was volume drained of its substance, immaterial and transparent. Thus there was no longer any obstacle to seeing another object through a solid. By the same token it was possible for the painter to dispose his planes at will, in a space that now had lost homogeneity and isotropy, there being no longer any need to arrange them in terms of their relative positions in space, between foreground

GEORGES BRAQUE (1882). THE ROOFTOPS, 1911.
COLLECTION OF MR AND MRS RALPH F. COLIN, NEW YORK.

and horizon line. The anti-illusionist quality of this new space was intensified in 1911 by the introduction of carefully executed lettering, sometimes stencilled on to the canvas. At a later date Braque explained that the purpose of including letters of the alphabet and numbers was to demonstrate by their purity and total absence of distortion that they were no longer governed by the laws of perspective. Their function was also to create stable planes serving so to speak as guide-marks, *points de repère*, in a space that, being no longer homogeneous, was no longer subject to fixed measurement.

For similar reasons color could no longer coincide with form and, given its independence, was not restricted to the natural color of the object. Not that the problem of local color was shelved, but in 1910 and 1911 it was subordinated—provisionally —to the more immediate demands of form. When, however, early in 1912, the two artists took to imitating textures, this question of local color came to the fore again. And could there be any better way of rendering the real color of, say, a violin, than by frankly reproducing the wood of which it was composed? Though in some cases exact imitation of the texture of the object was impracticable, certain substances, such as grained wood and marble, could be simulated with fair exactness, and Braque, son of a house-painter and decorator, devoted special care to these reproductions, seconded by a technique acquired in early youth.

The use of *papiers collés* was another outcome of the young artists' interest in local color. During this period manufacturers were turning out wallpaper that exactly imitated marble, wood-work and textiles, for the use of those who could not afford to employ such costly materials for the decoration of their homes. To save themselves the tedious task of painting imitations, at best approximative, of these materials, Picasso and Braque had the idea of applying strips of these wallpapers (which, being mechanically produced, had a finish hard to equal with their medium) directly to the canvas. Thus papers simulating grained wood, marble, floral tapestries and chair-caning were pasted, or simply pinned, to their pictures. Later, pieces of newspapers and matchboxes, postage stamps and visiting cards were added—objects whose typographical precision would have been hard to reproduce by hand.

In the result, these "pasted papers" acquired an absolute significance and value; as when the name of the newspaper served to conjure up in a still life the newspaper itself; or a fragment of the wrapper of a pack of tobacco, the pack itself. But the two painters were quick to see that these pieces of paper also gave rise to spatial relations of the highest interest. Thus a strip of newsprint or packing paper made it possible to bring forward or move back certain planes, by the interplay of values it created. This new procedure was skillfully employed in *Man's Head* (Tristan Tzara Collection, Paris), where there is no mistaking the way in which the blue paper in the center makes the plane of the face advance towards the beholder. By reason of their different dimensions and intensities of tone, this piece of paper and the fragment of newsprint on the left create two distinct planes at unequal distances from the head between them, with the result that this acquires, without any recourse to volumes, a density that mere linear design alone could not have given it.

Some critics, even well disposed ones, saw in these *papiers collés* a deliberate reversion to illusionist procedures and drew the conclusion that Picasso and Braque were trying by these means to regain touch with reality. Actually, however, *papiers collés* had nothing in common with traditional *trompe-l'œil* devices since the purpose behind their figurative aspects—we are not concerned here with spatial values—was not to create an optical illusion in terms of perspective, but to bring out one of the essential qualities of the object: a quality that is *per se* unaffected by atmospheric changes, spatial position, or variations of lighting; that permanent quality of the universal which lies behind appearances.

Here we have one of the distinctive characteristics of Cubism, markedly differentiating it from classical painting; the thing represented is never a specific object viewed under certain conditions, but a type-object whose attributes are found in each of its successive individuations. Differing from his predecessors, the Cubist does not represent a single, necessarily arbitrary aspect of the object, but seeks to reveal its basic, constant properties. Not that his standpoint is one of immaterialist idealism. True, in one of his essays on esthetics (*Sobre el punto de vista en las artes*, published in *Revista de Occidente*, February 1924) José Ortega y Gasset says that all painting subsequent to Cézanne depicts Ideas alone, and that while Ideas, too, are "objects," they are objects of a special kind, immanent in the subject and thus "intrasubjective." Cubism is idealist in the sense that it deals with *types*, but it is also and above all realistic, in the sense that it always keeps in close touch with the outside world. Though not a literal depiction, the cubist picture is an objective representation, and nothing could be more erroneous than to think the Cubist turns his back on nature.

Thus it is a great mistake to regard Cubism as a sort of abstract art indifferent to reality. Some, it is true, have seen in Cubism one of the final steps of a gradual movement towards abstraction and sought to account for the retention of figurative elements by talking of a sentimental fidelity to tradition or even of a certain sloth of mind. And provided all the later productions of Picasso and Braque are studiously ignored, this convenient "explanation" enables those who sponsor it to trace a plausible line of evolution leading to the painting of today;

PABLO PICASSO (1881). MAN'S HEAD, 1912-1913. PAPIER COLLÉ.
TRISTAN TZARA COLLECTION, PARIS.

PABLO PICASSO (1881). VIOLIN, 1912. PAPIER COLLÉ.
PRIVATE COLLECTION, PARIS.

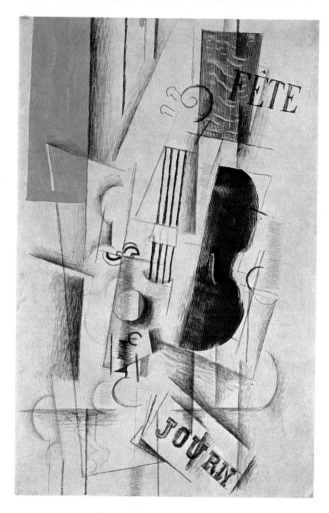

GEORGES BRAQUE (1882). MUSICAL FORMS, 1913. PAPIER COLLÉ.
PHILADELPHIA MUSEUM OF ART, ARENSBERG COLLECTION.

and this is all the easier since many of the modern tendencies towards abstraction, in fact, derive from Cubism. Yet, aside from the fact that these, as we shall see, are always *realistic* tendencies—precisely those which resolutely refuse to reduce non-figurative art to mere lyrical effusion—it must be pointed out, and emphasized, that neither Picasso nor Braque ever imagined that an unmeaning pattern of forms and colors, even if it contained a minimal number of allusions to reality, was enough to constitute a picture. In their art every line, every plane and every spatial relation has a realistic significance. Nor is there any question of a reconstruction or transposition of nature in terms of some sublime poetic vision transcending the everyday appearances of objects as seen by the normal eye. In cubist art there is nothing of romantic subjectivity or of super-reality; nor does it contain esoteric intimations of a metamorphosed world, as a certain school of poetic criticism would have us believe.

Should we, then, conclude that, while starting out from nature, Braque and Picasso distorted it out of recognition? There is a commonly held opinion that a long series of de-formations and re-formations culminated in the creation by the Cubists of a world where all is strange and nothing recognizable. On this view Cubism, though realistic in the sense of bodying forth reality as a whole, ended up with unreality, since it no longer concerned itself with reality as we see it. Here, it would seem, we come up against what is the crucial issue for an under-standing of Cubism, and it is the failure to grasp this point that has led to all the ambiguities and anomalies still found in apprai-sals of Cubism and, in a general way, of all modern painting. In brief, the great mistake consists in thinking that there is a "retinal vision," conformity with which leads to realism while its rejection leads to "unrealism"—a view that is tantamount to holding that the normal vision, i.e. our way of seeing the

outside world in everyday life, is identical with the classical
way of seeing sponsored by the Renaissance and subsequently
maintained with more or less success in academic art.

True, if it is taken for granted that the classical canons
exactly tally with the data furnished by reality and that reality
can be visualized only in terms of the traditional laws of

GEORGES BRAQUE (1882). TABLE WITH PIPE, 1913.
H. P. ROCHÉ COLLECTION, PARIS.

perspective and pictorial architecture, it follows that any infringement of these rules must necessarily diminish the realistic value of a work of art, and it must also be admitted that Cubism "deforms" nature. This holds good not only for Cubism but also for all forms of art prior to the Renaissance, since they, too, did not conform to the laws in question. But if, on the other hand, we grant that painting (and art in general) is a visual concretion of our knowledge of the outside world and expresses, not an immutable reality, but our experience and conceptions of a reality that is forever changing (or anyhow gives this impression, since we are perpetually discovering new aspects of it), and once we admit that the artist's choice of his plastic means is determined not by their purely imitative qualities but by their adequacy to the results of his observation of the world around him and to the values created by his cultural environment—then, surely, it is easy to see that Cubism, far from distorting nature, provides a new interpretation of it, equally realistic though other than that of the Renaissance.

In brief, the so-called illegibility of Picasso's and Braque's works is not due to their playing fast and loose with natural appearances, but to the fact that we try to "read" them in terms of obsolete conventions, instead of seeking to adjust our vision to the new conventions they inaugurated. As Pierre Francastel has aptly pointed out in his *Peinture et Société* (Audin, Lyons, 1951, p. 73), "Renaissance art is a system of conventional signs, meaningful only to those who have been initiated into the postulates of a culture embodying certain technical skills and beliefs. It is not directly accessible to the uninitiated; and a time has come when it no longer tallies with the discoveries of our present-day culture." That is why proposing to appraise a still life or *papier collé* of 1912—or for that matter any truly modern work—by classical criteria is like trying to translate a Chinese text with the help of a Greek dictionary.

GRIS AND MARCOUSSIS

BY 1905 or 1906, very soon, that is to say, after his arrival in Montmartre, Picasso had become the leading figure of a small group of artists, writers and more or less picturesque Bohemians who forgathered in cheap restaurants ("Chez Vernin," then "Chez Azon"), or in their studios—particularly Picasso's—or the humble lodgings up a squalid alley, not far from the Bateau Lavoir, where Max Jacob lived and entertained his friends every Monday. They soon came to be known to dwellers on the Butte Montmartre as *la bande à Picasso* (Picasso's gang), so evidently was he accepted as their leader, despite the many differences and idiosyncrasies of individual members of the group. Seeing him in the company of Derain, Braque, Apollinaire and Salmon, Gertrude Stein remarked that he reminded her of Napoleon followed by four enormous grenadiers, and, she added, "Picasso was every inch a chief" (see *Autobiography of Alice B. Toklas*).

Not that the group had the appearance of a clan, still less a coterie all adoration for a deeply venerated Master. Its members, indeed, had little in common between them except their poverty. The artists, in particular, had usually quite conflicting aspirations and most of those who witnessed the initial phase of Cubism followed Picasso's experiments with more curiosity than approbation. Manolo and Vlaminck greeted his canvases with guffaws, while most of the others observed a prudent skepticism. Even Derain refused to commit himself. At this early stage Braque was the only member of the group to appreciate the exceptional interest of the young Spaniard's discoveries and their significance for the future of art. Before long, however, two other painters threw in their lot with the new esthetic, and frankly, without any striving after spurious originality, followed the trail blazed by Picasso.

63

JUAN GRIS (1887-1927). HOMAGE TO PICASSO, 1912.
COLLECTION OF MR AND MRS LEIGH B. BLOCK, CHICAGO.

JUAN GRIS (1887-1927). THREE CARDS, 1913.
HERMANN RUPF COLLECTION, BERN.

A compatriot of Picasso and six years his junior, Juan Gris had settled in Paris in 1906. Attracted by the rising prestige of the elder artist, he had made haste to secure a small studio in the Bateau Lavoir that had just been vacated by Kees van Dongen. By a curious coincidence he moved in just when Picasso was starting work on *Les Demoiselles d'Avignon*. Thus he was present at the birth of Cubism and could follow its evolution from the first tentative manifestations. However, he did not participate in it at once, since he was almost penniless and, instead of devoting himself to painting, had to earn his living by making humorous cartoons for illustrated periodicals: *L'Assiette au Beurre, Le Charivari, Le Cri de Paris*.

When at last, in 1911, Gris was free to follow his own bent, he did not try to make up for lost time by plunging at once into Analytical Cubism as practised by Picasso and Braque. A cautious artist, of a reflective turn of mind, he preferred to start by testing for himself certain cubist procedures, without blindly committing himself to the idiom of his precursors. In a series of canvases, best known of which is the portrait of his friend Maurice Raynal, he applied himself to studying the problems set by light striking on the volumes of objects or bodies, and carefully noting the play of broken gleams and their effects, sometimes dissolvent, sometimes constructive, on masses and outlines. Fortified by the knowledge thus acquired, he moved on to a system of pictorial construction in which oblique, parallel rays of light gave rise to simple, clean-cut forms somewhat rigid in appearance.

Still Life with a Guitar (Museum of Modern Art, New York) and the 1912 portrait of Picasso, modestly entitled *Homage to Picasso*, are among the most representative works of this period. In them the delicacy and luminosity of the colors more than compensate for the occasional traces of stylization (due to an evident desire for integral plasticity) which he had not yet

JUAN GRIS (1887-1927). THE WASH-BASIN, 1912.
COLLECTION OF THE VICOMTESSE DE NOAILLES, PARIS.

learnt to eliminate. Although as a rule these canvases are readily comprehensible, we find procedures directly stemming from Picasso's Cubism: notably tiltings of planes and partial variations of the viewpoint. We also find in *Still Life with a Guitar* some departures from the scale of dimensions prescribed by classical perspective, and these go to show that the intrinsic value of the object already meant more to Gris than the figurative verisimilitude of monocular vision. Though he was one of the few Cubists not to pass through a Cézannesque phase (in the full sense of the term), the course of his researches was to lead him, no less logically than the others, to that Analytical Cubism intimations of which can be discerned in the canvases of the winter of 1911-1912.

There is, however, a sharp distinction between his analytical works and those preceding them; a difference so marked that one might almost speak of two separate "manners," his pre-cubist and his cubist manner, for example. Many years later Gris was to declare that he did not deliberately take to Cubism; he merely worked in "a state of mind" that led him to be classed amongst the exponents of that tendency (see his statement in the questionnaire titled *Chez les Cubistes, Bulletin de la Vie Artistique*, January 1, 1925). Naturally we can take his word for this, but it is an undoubted fact that once Gris had decided to employ the analytical technique he never looked back. Noteworthy, too, is the fact that, while learning much from Picasso, he resolutely followed the call of his own temperament and diverged at several points from the path mapped out by the great pioneer. For though Gris employed several viewpoints simultaneously, he took pains to ensure the visual plausibility of every aspect of the object, and always refused to dissociate color from form. But it was color with a difference, wholly independent of "local color" properly so called, and he could thus indulge in vivid, sometimes strongly contrasted tonalities. Generally he contents himself with a sort of pictorial sample of the textures figuring on the canvas—wood, marble and so forth; however, in the case of objects refractory to analysis, such as mirrors, engravings, or reproductions of pictures, he inserts them boldly, as such, in the composition.

Finally, whereas Picasso and Braque gave more thought to the qualities of the object than to the actual structure of the picture, Gris subordinates the various representative elements to an exceptionally rigorous architectonic concept. Independently of its significant value, each part is dovetailed into the composition with minute precision and with an eye to the picture's organic unity. While we must admit that some of his 1912 canvases may seem a little dry or theory-ridden, *Three Cards* (Hermann Rupf Collection, Bern) and *Violin and Guitar* (Ralph Colin Collection, New York) unquestionably rank among the major achievements of Cubism.

Louis Markous, a Polish artist, whose name Apollinaire frenchified into "Marcoussis" (the name of a small village near Paris), followed much the same path as Juan Gris. He too had no private means and had to earn his living by making cartoons for periodicals. In 1910 he came in touch with Braque and was much taken by his work. Though in the series of townscapes which he painted shortly afterwards, such as *The Sacré Cœur* (1911), we find few traces of Braque's influence, they make clear Marcoussis' keen interest in architecturally ordered structure. Volumes are fully rendered and bathed in an all-pervading light that softly models forms, but also gives line an intrinsic value, often detaching it from the mass it circumscribes. More orthodox, from the cubist standpoint, are the etchings he made in 1911 and 1912, several of which figured at the "Section d'Or" exhibition. While some, notably the *Portrait of M. Grabovski*, testify to the artist's intensive study of volumes, the *Portrait of M. Gazanion* and, above all, *La Belle Martiniquaise*, though

LOUIS MARCOUSSIS (1883-1941). THE MUSICIAN, 1914.
NATIONAL GALLERY OF ART, WASHINGTON, D.C., CHESTER DALE COLLECTION.

in a general way highly personal in conception, also contain "passages" and tilted planes obviously deriving from the technique practised by Picasso and Braque.

Less original, perhaps, was Marcoussis' analytical period. *Pyrogène* and, in particular, the large still life in the Musée d'Art Moderne in Paris—both date to 1912—wholly conform to the practices of the founders of Cubism. The execution of *Bar du Port* (1913) is more independent, but the content has, perhaps, less substantiality. *The Musician* (Chester Dale Collection, National Gallery of Art, Washington), exhibited in the 1914 Salon des Indépendants, marks the climactic point of the artist's pre-war production. For Marcoussis was now beginning to shake off earlier influences and moving towards that subtler mode of expression, charged with poetic intimations, which was to characterize his art after 1920.

In this survey of the Montmartre Cubists it would be unjust to omit the name of Auguste Herbin, an uneven painter but one of unquestionable probity. Though living in the Bateau Lavoir, he kept severely to himself and never mixed with the Picasso group. Nevertheless it would seem that he kept track of the discoveries and inventions of Picasso, since, after having been drawn to Fauvism and "Cézannism," he developed, from 1911 on, a style of painting patently influenced by that of his illustrious neighbor. But after a phase of Analytical Cubism in the following years he gradually tended—regrettably in our opinion—towards a thoroughgoing stylization that in some respects foreshadowed his non-figurative period, though this did not prevent his lapsing, after the war, into a neo-realism at the furthest possible remove from Cubism.

PABLO PICASSO (1881). THE BOTTLE OF SUZE, 1913.
WASHINGTON UNIVERSITY, ST. LOUIS, MO.

SYNTHETIC CUBISM

W HILE the year 1910 had decisive consequences on the course of all contemporary painting, 1913 witnessed a no less significant turning-point in that of Cubism. Now, however, it was not the painter's technique, in the positive sense of the term, that was revised and renovated, but his manner of conceiving the relations between subject and object; in other words, the whole "method" of his art. The task the Cubists set themselves in 1910 had been that of inaugurating a wholly novel vision of the world by creating new practical means of expression; now, however, in 1913, they turned to a more intellectual form of investigation, bearing on the manner in which the painter apprehends the objects that he represents. More exactly, the question was one of examining the repercussions that various modes of apprehension have on the plastic aspects of the image. In short, the formal revolution now was succeeded by one of a psychological order, and it is not surprising that this latter attracted less attention than the former and that many art historians have seen in it an episode of merely secondary importance.

It must also be noted that the transition from one form of art to the other took place gradually—even more gradually perhaps than that of 1910—and that the change from any given work to its immediate successor is often hardly perceptible. Yet when we compare a canvas of the winter of 1912-1913 with one of the following winter, the differences are evident, chiefly in the case of Picasso; for Braque's evolution now was decidedly slower and also went slightly less deep.

When we study Picasso's works in chronological order, what strikes us most perhaps is the reappearance of pure and brilliant color, strongly contrasting with the rigorous austerity of Analytical Cubism. The blue oval in *Bottle of Suze* (Washington

University, St. Louis) and the red rectangle on the label of the bottle are a veritable feast for the eyes after the grisailles of the *Portrait of Kahnweiler* and *The Poet*. But on scrutinizing with some attention works of this kind, we cannot fail to notice the almost complete disappearance of "analytical" complexities and a marked simplification of the figures.

It must be admitted that, brilliant as were its achievements, Analytical Cubism was somewhat restricted in its scope. Subsequently Juan Gris himself, with characteristic honesty and lucidity, formulated some of its shortcomings. Chiefly he blamed it for having led to representation of a purely descriptive order, since in Analytical Cubism "the only comprehensive relations that continued to exist were those between the painter and objects; hardly ever those between the objects themselves" (*Bulletin de la Vie Artistique*, January 1, 1925). This opinion may err on the side of severity, but there is no question that the manner of representation prevailing in 1911-1912 went perilously near sacrificing the unity of the object to fidelity to fact. By freeing the object from the limitations of classical perspective, Picasso had succeeded in making a completer, more faithful image of it, but in so doing he had disrupted its homogeneity. If the object were not to end up as a mere assemblage of lines wholly without density, it was high time to restore its inner cohesion. But any attempts in this direction were bound to be frustrated by the method of empirical observation basic to Analytical Cubism, while any synthesis of the formal elements involved the risk of insidiously re-introducing "Renaissance" space into the picture, by way of volumes.

As, three years previously, Picasso had learnt to dispense with models, so in the course of 1913 he gradually discovered that he no longer needed directly to observe the objects that he proposed to reproduce. In particular he realized that, instead of sorting out in his mind the qualities of a given object,

PABLO PICASSO (1881). GIRL'S HEAD, 1913.
PRIVATE COLLECTION, PARIS.

basing his selection on "constants" revealed by previous experimentation, he could quite as well—indeed, to better effect—figure out the essentials of its pictorial representation *a priori,* provided this representation stemmed from a lucid, logical understanding of the specific nature of the object. In other words his new method was to penetrate, by an act of intuition, into the essence of the object and thus to discover its basic characteristics, those that conditioned its very being, and lacking which it would not be what it is. And the next step, after getting these preliminary data clearly established in his mind, was to integrate them into a single image, constituting as it were the pictorial essence of the object. The resulting picture would thus contain, potentially, all possible individuations of the object. And so, from the type-object, he now moved on to the principle-object, to the essential entity.

We need only compare the glass in the *Still Life with Bottle of Maraschino* (1914) with the glasses in such analytical works as *L'Indépendant* or *Still Life with "Le Journal"* of 1912, to see how thoroughly the object has now regained its plastic unity. Instead of being a heterogeneous assemblage of fragments of contour lines, the glass is rendered by a simple profile and concentric circles, expressing at once its form and volume. Stripped of accidentals and reduced to essential predicates, it becomes the *principle* of the glass. Moreover, since color is an eminently variable attribute, it now is independent of the object and therefore liberated from the servitudes of "local tone."

All the same, simulated fabrics and actual paper fragments were still employed; but Picasso now treated them with far greater freedom. The former were no longer scrupulously exact facsimiles; some simple "allusions" in the choice and handling of colors sufficed to suggest them. Likewise *papiers collés* lost more and more their documentary significance and now became almost exclusively (but with more flexibility than heretofore)

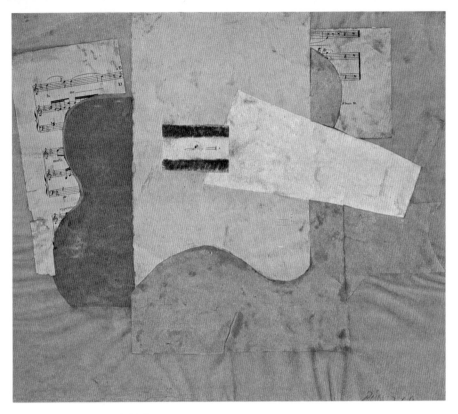

PABLO PICASSO (1881). SHEET OF MUSIC AND GUITAR, WINTER 1912-1913.
PAPIER COLLÉ. GEORGES SALLES COLLECTION, PARIS.

a primordial means for the expression of space. Very likely it
was through using them for this purpose that Picasso came to
understand the purely relative value of local tones. In the course
of using pieces of paper of miscellaneous colors he must have
noticed that the object was rendered quite as well as before

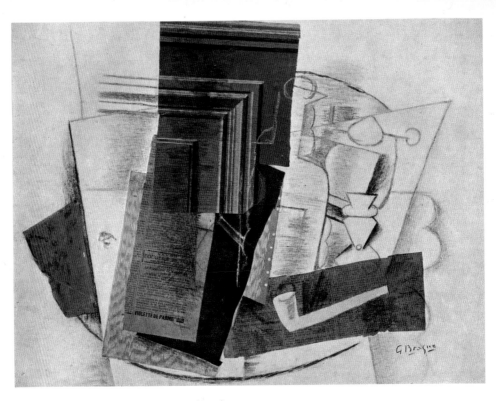

GEORGES BRAQUE (1882). BOTTLE, GLASS AND PIPE, 1914.
COLLECTION OF LADY HULTON, LONDON.

—"qualified," as Juan Gris was later to describe it. Such a work
as *Sheet of Music and Guitar* (Georges Salles Collection, Paris),
made in the winter of 1912-1913—that is to say in a period
when local color still reigned supreme—is highly significant
in this respect. The strips of white and ochre paper on a blue
ground have no relation to the actual texture or color of the

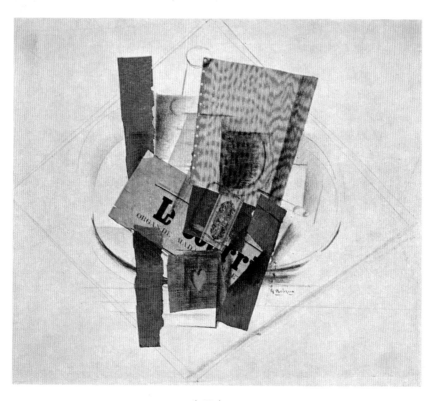

GEORGES BRAQUE (1882). LE COURRIER, 1913.
PHILADELPHIA MUSEUM OF ART, GALLATIN COLLECTION.

instrument; nevertheless the object had never yet been interpreted with so much fidelity to fact and such purity of conception, combined with such thoroughgoing plastic economy of
means. Notwithstanding its small dimensions, this collage
constitutes a landmark in the development of Cubism; indeed
it strikes the keynote of the new pictorial language.

Braque's evolution, as has been pointed out, was more tardy. The *Table with Pipe* (Roché Collection, Paris) is still entirely analytical, and the same is true of some of his works of early 1914. It would seem that the artist's chief preoccupation in 1913 was with exploiting the spatial possibilities of *papiers collés* and that, as a result, he tended somewhat to neglect the representative values of the picture content. Thus in *Le Courrier* (Gallatin Collection) the object has only secondary importance and it is the creation of space by superimposed planes that catches our attention. And the result of this characteristic disposition of the planes, so frequent in his works of this period, was considerably to defer the reunification of the plastic image. Thus in *Aria de Bach* (though this is certainly one of Braque's best works) there is still an undeniable lack of homogeneity in the structure of the guitar. Indeed it is not until the still lifes of 1918-1920 that we find the object regaining an entire cohesion. Similarly it was only after the war had ended that Braque definitely broke free from the thrall of local color; generally speaking, his works of 1913-1914 are only slightly colored, and color is almost always subordinated to the physical properties of the object.

In this respect the art of Juan Gris underwent a much more rapid evolution. True, his study of the problem of spatial values was less acute than Braque's and he did not carry it so far. All the same, the progress he made in a single year was quite remarkable. In his *papiers collés* of 1914, in particular, he attained a purity of expression coupled with a plastic rigor that is wholly admirable. Like Picasso, though never directly inspired by him, he reduced objects to their essential attributes and with these composed intelligible, coherent renderings of them, slightly more idealized perhaps than those of the elder artist. But most noteworthy in his compositions are the ever-increasing solidity of their structure and the extreme care with which Gris prepares and assembles each element within an overall architectonic

GEORGES BRAQUE (1882). OVAL STILL LIFE, 1914.
MUSEUM OF MODERN ART, NEW YORK.

schema. Yet these technical preoccupations do not hamper in any way the expression of a delicately poetic imagination. On the contrary, far from impoverishing the general effect, the simplification of forms and elimination of all superfluous details in such works as *Cup and Roses* and *The Bottle of Banyuls* enhance their purity and clarity.

After effecting two drastic revolutions within a space of under five years, Cubism might have been expected to settle down and achieve a stable equilibrium. Now that the major problems tackled by the painters had been fully solved, some contemporaries believed that, having come to the end of a surprisingly prolific and rapid evolution, Cubism would now become stabilized and give birth to a "style"—much as the classicism of the 16th and 17th centuries followed the experimental art of the 15th century. But Cubism was not destined to crystallize into a set formula, however alluring. The new intuitive approach had opened up so many hitherto undreamt-of possibilities and so wide a field of imagery, that it was bound to lead to new developments. Thus, though Cubism's creative and formative phase came to an end in 1914, it still had much to give the future.

However, as a result of the outbreak of the Great War, it underwent a temporary eclipse. With Braque mobilized and Picasso and Gris isolated from their colleagues, plowing a lonely furrow, a break in the continuity of the movement was inevitable. A break all the more conspicuous since Picasso, though he did not abandon Cubism, dallied with other forms of art in 1915 and above all 1917, when he began to paint sets for Diaghilev's Russian Ballet. Aside from Picasso's seeming defection, other incidents such as the sale of Kahnweiler's property after the war led many to think that Cubism was in a decline and retreating from the hard-won vantage-point it had occupied in the years immediately before the war.

GEORGES BRAQUE (1882). ARIA DE BACH, 1914.
PRIVATE COLLECTION, PARIS.

For, while still lacking widespread recognition, the Cubists had enjoyed the support of a small but steadily increasing body of admirers and connoisseurs. Some new collectors, for the most part foreigners, such as Dr Vincenc Kramar (of Prague) and Alfred Flechtheim (of Düsseldorf), had joined the ranks of their earliest patrons, and the prices fetched by cubist works were rising appreciably. This was particularly the case with Picasso, whose large canvas, *Family of Saltimbanques* (Chester Dale Collection, National Gallery, Washington), masterpiece of his Pink Period, fetched no less than 11,500 francs—a very large sum for the time—at the auction sale held in the Hôtel Drouot, Paris, March 2, 1914. For appreciation of the new esthetic was no longer confined to an understanding few; it was beginning to interest a wider public, all who wanted to keep abreast of the latest fashion, notable among the "popularizers" of Cubism being the famous couturier Paul Poiret. However, the Cubists were only too glad to leave the task of championing their cause to the little band of critics who understood their works, several of whom were wildly enthusiastic. Cubism certainly owed much to their efforts, even though none was of the caliber of a Baudelaire and some thought fit to credit the artists with far-fetched notions that had never crossed their heads, thus giving them the (quite unjustified) reputation of being theory-ridden doctrinaires. Their most doughty and determined champions were Maurice Raynal, André Salmon and above all Guillaume Apollinaire, who put their gifts as writers and lecturers at the service of the cubist cause.

A Bohemian in easy circumstances, a brilliant if relatively unprolific writer, Raynal, besides being one of its chroniclers, was so fervent an advocate of the movement that he was sometimes accused of pressing his enthusiasm too far. Actually, however, his activities were usually discreet and did little to catch the public eye, though he came boldly into the open in

1912 on the occasion of the "Section d'Or" exhibition. André Salmon, after being strictly non-committal, even hostile, to begin with, valiantly defended Cubism from 1911 on in *Paris Journal*, to which under the pen name "La Palette" he contributed a *Courrier des Ateliers*, in which he spoke not only of what was "doing" in the artists' studios but also of art

PABLO PICASSO (1881). STILL LIFE WITH A BOTTLE OF MARASCHINO, 1914. PRIVATE COLLECTION, PARIS.

in general. When in May 1912 he changed over to *Gil Blas*, he did much to counteract the activities of Louis Vauxcelles, sworn foe of all avant-garde art. It was Salmon who, on leaving *L'Intransigeant* two years earlier, had arranged for Apollinaire to be taken on the staff. Wildly enthusiastic for all things modern, Apollinaire converted the newspaper owned by that staunch conservative Léon Bailby into the principal organ for the defense of Cubism. All went well until 1914 when, taken to task by a colleague for his encomium of one of Archipenko's sculptures, he resigned his post.

The activities of these art critics were not confined to daily papers. All were looking around for a periodical in which they could air their views, and a first opportunity was provided by Ricciotto Canudo, a writer of Italian origin and a champion of so-called "cerebrist" art, who early in 1913 launched an illustrated magazine named *Montjoie!* (oddly subtitled "Organ of French Artistic Imperialism"). Apollinaire and Salmon covered the various Salons and the magazine featured articles by vanguard artists, amongst them Gleizes and Léger, as well as reproductions of cubist pictures.

All the same *Montjoie!* was too eclectic in its policy to satisfy Apollinaire, who made it a point of honor to be always in the extreme forefront of the modernist movement. Then two of his many friends, Serge Jastrebzoff and his sister Hélène d'Oettingen, offered him the post of joint editor of a little literary magazine *Soirées de Paris* which, launched by André Billy in 1912, was on the point of foundering. Jastrebzoff, one of Picasso's warmest admirers and himself a cubist painter (under the pseudonym of Férat), and his sister, a highly gifted author, approved wholeheartedly of Apollinaire's views on art. Early in the winter of 1913-1914 they bought out Billy's interest in *Soirées* and made of it a vehicle for the propagation of the new esthetic and in particular of Cubism. Owing to the outbreak of war this

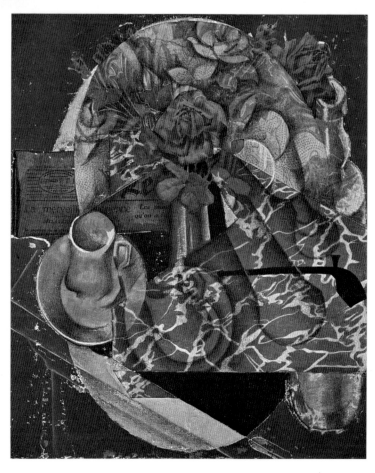

JUAN GRIS (1887-1927). CUP AND ROSES, 1914.
PRIVATE COLLECTION, PARIS.

JUAN GRIS (1887-1927). THE BOTTLE OF BANYULS, 1914.
HERMANN RUPF COLLECTION, BERN.

second avatar of the magazine was short-lived; but it survived long enough to have much influence on the literary and artistic life of Paris.

As a matter of fact the higher type of journalism suited Apollinaire better than the task of essayist and art historian which he assumed in 1913, when he wrote *Les Peintres Cubistes*. It is regrettable that this work was so long regarded, and is still sometimes regarded, as a sort of gospel or codification of cubist theory—which, incidentally, was not its author's intention when he wrote it. The first part, "Esthetic Meditations," consisted merely of more or less verbatim reproductions of articles already published; when read individually they gave the effect of agreeably poetic essays, but their assemblage in a book revealed the slightness, not to say the weakness of their esthetic content. There is no question that Apollinaire had taste and no little flair, but both were purely instinctive and, despite the beauty of the style, the "meditations" have only a remote connection with art —and a still remoter one with Cubism. And the second part, a series of studies, varying in quality, of the cubist painters, reflected far more Apollinaire's personal ideas of each of them than their actual intentions.

Moreover, his classification—long deemed authoritative— of the various cubist tendencies hardly corresponded to the facts, though it evinced a wholly laudable desire on the author's part to create a sort of "common front" of modern painting. An admirer and the earliest champion of Cubism as practised by Picasso and Braque, Apollinaire could not fail to notice the numerous tendencies and parallel developments to which the original movement had given birth. The project of uniting all on a wide front, though it surprised and even shocked some of his friends, seems to have been amply justified by the event and may probably be regarded as the chief merit of Apollinaire's *Peintres Cubistes*.

ROBERT DELAUNAY (1885-1941). RED EIFFEL TOWER, 1911.
SOLOMON R. GUGGENHEIM MUSEUM, NEW YORK.

THE EXHIBITORS IN ROOM 41

Though the type of Cubism created by Picasso and Braque and practised, after them, by Gris and Marcoussis embodied a consistent esthetic, may conveniently be regarded as central to the movement and might indeed be described as the criterion of cubist orthodoxy, there is no denying that the tendency represented by these four artists is far from covering all the developments of Cubism in its widest sense. True, there can be no question of lumping together in the same category all the contemporary manifestations of vanguard art, but it would be equally unrealistic to dissociate from the movement this or that trend, this or that artist, simply because they deviate from Cubism's original conception. Cubism was not in any sense a "school" employing one and the same idiom; the term covers a host of ventures both divergent and converging. For the initial stimulus given by Picasso and Braque in the years 1908-1910 inaugurated a whole series of experiments, and while some of the artists concerned followed in the footsteps of the two great pioneers, others, more original, struck out in new directions and opened new horizons. Thus, while we must be careful not to underrate the achievement of the two painters who laid the foundations of the new art, we should do wrong to overlook the contributions, sometimes no less creative, made by other artists who added luster to the movement.

For, historically speaking, the consequence of Braque's and Picasso's abstention from exhibiting in the Salons was that it was left to other painters to bring Cubism to the notice of the public at large. Though critics and discriminating connoisseurs had already been aware of its existence, it was not until the opening of the 1911 Salon des Indépendants that it came to rank, in the eyes of connoisseurs and public, as a movement of prime importance. This, the twenty-seventh exhibition of that name, was far from being expected to flutter the artistic dovecotes and the Press agreed in predicting a sharp decline in "eccentricities." These reassuring forecasts made the shock all the greater when unsuspecting visitors entered that famous "Room 41." The artists showing in it were Jean Metzinger *(Landscape, Woman's Head* and *Still Life)*, Albert Gleizes *(Male Nude, Woman with Phlox* and two landscapes*)*, Le Fauconnier *(Abundance* and *Portrait of Paul Castiaux)*, Fernand Léger *(Nudes in a Landscape)* and Robert Delaunay (three scenes of Paris including *City No. 2* and *The Eiffel Tower*).

Though different tendencies could be seen in the works presented in Room 41, all had this in common: that volumes and pictorial architecture were stressed at the expense of color— for which reason all five artists were unanimously labeled "Cubists" by the Press. By the same token Cubism, hitherto the apanage of two artists who deliberately shunned publicity, now created something of a scandal and gave rise to heated controversies. There were angry protests on the opening day, and thereafter Room 41 was always thronged with derisive or indignant groups of visitors, loudly declaring that they could not make head or tail of these absurd "picture puzzles," whose subjects, whatever these might be, were buried under a mass of cubes. Most professional critics were either hostile or discreetly disapproving. Delaunay's *Tower*, in particular, was a target for ironical comments. In the *Petit Parisien* of April 23, 1911, a journalist described it as "an Eiffel Tower toppled over, presumably with an eye to destroying the nearby houses which, dancing a cancan, are rudely sticking their chimney pots into each other's windows." Guillaume Apollinaire alone (in *L'Intransigeant*, April 21, 1911) vigorously defended the painters now under fire from all quarters. "We are witnessing," he wrote, "the rise of an art of spareness and sobriety, whose still somewhat rigid aspects will very soon be humanized."

In June of that year the Cercle des Indépendants at Brussels invited the same artists to exhibit some of their works at its Salon and asked Apollinaire to contribute a preface to the catalogue. In it he accepted, on their behalf, the name "Cubists," but sensibly pointed out that Cubism was not a cut-and-dried system: "the marked differences, not only of talent but also of manner, in the works of these artists make that clear."

The Salon d'Automne opened its doors at Paris on September 30, 1911. To the chagrin of the new men's adversaries, the selection committee showed itself much more broad-minded than it had been three years before in the case of Braque. Georges Desvallières, its chairman, carried impartiality to the point of allotting a special gallery, Room VIII, to the Cubists. Most commented on were Gleizes' *Portrait of Jacques Nayral* and *The Hunt*, Metzinger's *Tea Time* (christened by André Salmon, a little later, "Cubism's *Monna Lisa*"), three landscapes by Le Fauconnier, and Léger's *Essai pour trois portraits*.

The reactions of the public were even more hostile than at the Indépendants. Though defended by Apollinaire, by Roger Allard in *La Cote* and by André Warnod in *Comoedia*, the Cubists were subjected to attacks from all the rest of the Press. Thus Louis Vauxcelles, writing in *Gil Blas*, described Cubism as "the sort of art and ideology that would have delighted Père Ubu." Needless to say, none of the critics troubled to note the differences between the various artists; all that caught their eye was the geometric aspect common to their works; as when Régis Gignoux declared that "conforming to the same theories and technique, they render all their subjects indiscriminately in the form of cubes" (*Le Figaro*, September 24, 1911).

There is, of course, no doubt that all five artists exhibiting in Room 41 had been led to Cubism by a study of the problems set by volumes. All the same, the tendencies that Metzinger, Gleizes and Le Fauconnier stood for must be distinguished from

ALBERT GLEIZES (1881-1953). MAN ON BALCONY, 1912.
PHILADELPHIA MUSEUM OF ART, ARENSBERG COLLECTION.

JEAN METZINGER (1883-1957). TEA TIME, 1911.
PHILADELPHIA MUSEUM OF ART, ARENSBERG COLLECTION.

those of Léger and Delaunay whose modes of expression,
though at this stage resembling those of other members of the
group, soon became much more personal and original.

Born at Nantes in 1883, Jean Metzinger had come under the influence of Neo-Impressionism shortly after his arrival in Paris. His *Portrait of Guillaume Apollinaire*, exhibited in 1910 at the Salon des Indépendants—Apollinaire was much exaggerating when he subsequently described it as "the first cubist portrait" —evidenced a new will to architectonic composition, but his authentically cubist period began only a little later, with a *Nude* exhibited in the Salon d'Automne of the same year. In this Picasso's influence was paramount, so much so that some critics accused Metzinger of downright plagiarism. And in fact this *Nude* was more "cubist" in the strict sense of the term than the works he turned out in the following year, such as *Portrait of Madame Metzinger* and *Tea Time*, where the fragmentation of volumes was far less thoroughgoing and "passages" were seldom or never used. Many years after, speaking of his 1911 works, Metzinger wrote: "I was trying at the time to break up natural volumes into planes that, by variations in their location, lighting and dimensions, would enable the spectator mentally to reconstruct those volumes and picture to himself the solid object existing in space." As a matter of fact the volumes in these works are still highly compact and self-contained; it is above all the lighting that makes known their relative positions, causing the most brightly lit planes to seem nearest the spectator. Moreover he was less concerned with observing objects than with the structure of the picture as a whole. "What he insists on," Gleizes has written in his *Souvenirs* (p. 24), "is that all the parts of his work shall tally with each other logically and justify each other down to the smallest detail; that the composition shall be an organic whole as strictly ordered as possible, with all 'accidental' elements of perception ruled out or, anyhow, kept under control... I frankly admit," Gleizes adds, "that I found these austere intellectual disciplines uncongenial at the time."

JEAN METZINGER (1883-1957). THE BATHERS, 1913.
PHILADELPHIA MUSEUM OF ART, ARENSBERG COLLECTION.

ALBERT GLEIZES (1881-1953). LADY WITH ANIMALS, 1914.
PEGGY GUGGENHEIM COLLECTION, VENICE.

His elder by two years, Gleizes had made Metzinger's acquaintance at one of the evening parties given by his friend the poet Alexandre Mercereau, but had felt much more drawn to another young man who often attended these gatherings, Henri Le Fauconnier, who, as far back as 1909, had fired him with a desire to turn aside from the beaten track of Post-Impressionism. Already in 1910 the canvases he sent to the Salon des Indépendants were distinguished by his use of large masses and the sobriety of the colors, but it was only at the end of the year that he faced up to the problem of volumes in his *Male Nude* and *Woman with Phlox*, which along with the *Portrait of Jacques Nayral* and *The Hunt* are the works most representative of Gleizes' Cubism in its Cézannesque phase. Here, less austere than Metzinger, he confined himself to simplifying forms of objects, schematizing outlines, and still showed much concern for details. If we may venture to coin yet another neologism on a theme that has already given rise to so many, we might say that he "cubistifies" (*fait cubiquer* was Apollinaire's term) classical, not to say academic subjects.

We find the same tendency towards "arranging" rather than "composing" in the work of Le Fauconnier, whose brief venture into Cubism was of a rather personal order. Though, as with Gleizes, the subject is predominant, this artist's aim was different, that of achieving a sort of impressionist Cubism. For, while clearly stated, volumes are rendered less for their own sake than in terms of the light that makes them iridescent, as well as modeling them; thus in *Abundance* we find a haze of broken lights, curiously impressionistic in effect. Le Fauconnier never advanced beyond this early stage, but soon turned towards a species of Expressionism, wholly different in spirit.

Despite the fact that Gleizes and Metzinger always denied it, there can be no question of the influence of Picasso and Braque on their art, also on Le Fauconnier's, although their solutions of similar problems differed in some respects. The two Montmartre painters regarded volumes, lighting and color as closely implicated, with the result that the modification of any one of these elements led sooner or later to that of the others. In the work of Gleizes and his friends they were always kept relatively independent. When, for example, color was sparely used, this was solely because the painter was aiming at austerity. Moreover light, especially in the work of Gleizes and Le Fauconnier, still played its classical part as a means of rendering space and imparting atmospheric unity to the composition. Most characteristic of their type of Cubism, however, was the retention of the anecdotal theme; to their mind, the predominance of the object over the subject sufficed to ensure the authenticity of the work as a whole. Even when at the end of 1912 Metzinger and Gleizes embarked on Analytical Cubism, they kept to this procedure. In their case, the use of numerous viewpoints did not lead to the creation of new pictorial signs, but merely gave an added liveliness to the subject by a fragmentation of its aspects. Gleizes himself described his Analytical period as "an analysis of the subject-image and the subject-scene." We need only study with some attention Metzinger's *Bathers* and *Blue Bird* (1913) and Gleizes' *Treading out the Corn* (1912) and *Lady with Animals* (1914) to perceive that, appearances notwithstanding, these works keep dutifully to the methods of classical pictorial architecture.

To sum up: this type of Cubism produces less the impression of a genuinely revolutionary form of expression than one of a call to order or a régime of austerity. It reaffirms the primacy of the painting itself over its anecdotal or emotive content, but without wholly abandoning the spatial and figurative system deriving from the Renaissance. Léger and Delaunay, however, took a very different view of this subordination of the subject to purely pictorial values. Though the subject did not, to their thinking, constitute a major obstacle to a wholly new vision, they saw no need to continue to present it in the traditional spatial frame of reference.

Son of a stock-breeder, first a draftsman in an architect's office, then employed as retoucher by a photographer, Fernand Léger was a much less cultivated young man than Gleizes or Metzinger and had no trouble in breaking with the disciplines

FERNAND LÉGER (1881-1955). NUDES IN THE FOREST, 1909-1910. RIJKSMUSEUM KRÖLLER-MÜLLER, OTTERLO.

of a conventional training. Though he studied (briefly) under Gérome and Gabriel Ferrier, he preferred to count, for the most part, on himself for the shaping of his vision. In revolt against academic art, which profoundly bored him, he began by turning towards the Impressionists, and he always acknowledged his debt to that liberation of pure color which was one of their achievements. It was Cézanne, however, who pointed him to the path he was to follow. Cézanne's influence, if not compulsive, was deep-seated, so much so that later in life Léger declared that it took him three full years to shake it off. "Over a long period I was guided by his work. He was always at my side. I never ceased exploring, making discoveries. Cézanne taught me to love forms and volumes, he bade me concentrate on drawing. It was then I had a presentiment that my drawing must be rigid, quite unsentimental" (see *Fernand Léger Catalogue*, p. 76, Musée des Arts Décoratifs, Paris 1956).

We have little documentation for this period, since Léger subsequently destroyed many of his early works; however, *The Seamstress* (c. 1910) and the famous *Nudes in the Forest* (1909-1910) seem to mark the culmination of this phase. "To the best of my ability," Léger tells us, "I went to the antipodes of Impressionism. I had an obsession; I was set on 'disjointing' bodies. You know what they called me: a 'tubist.' It was far from being plain sailing; I spent two whole years tussling with volume in *Nudes in the Forest*, which I completed in 1910. I wanted to stress volumes to their extreme limit. People have told me they see the Douanier's influence in this picture. That may well be true—I was in touch with the Douanier at the time—but, if so, I was influenced unconsciously. *Nudes in the Forest* meant to me solely a battlefield of volumes. I felt I could not make color do the job; volume was enough for me" (ib. p. 78). This work would come fairly close to those of Braque and Picasso (in 1908), were it not that its volumes are

FERNAND LÉGER (1881-1955). THE WEDDING, 1910-1911.
MUSÉE D'ART MODERNE, PARIS.

FERNAND LÉGER (1881-1955). WOMAN IN BLUE (SECOND STATE), 1912.
KUNSTMUSEUM, BASEL.

much more independent of each other. Léger violently "disjoints" them so as to affirm their individual existence and also to set up a sort of dynamic antagonism between them.

This will to dynamism, which was to characterize Léger's art up to the end, led him to introduce into his compositions "contrasts of forms." These made their first appearance at the beginning of 1911, their purpose being to play off with the utmost intensity large tracts of flat surfaces against the disjointed volumes of his previous period. In *The Smokers*, the smoke of the pipes flattens out in light-hued planes, their edges only very slightly modeled, contrasting with the deep recession of the landscape. In *The Wedding* and *Woman in Blue* the areas of flat color cease to have any figurative referents and are purely dynamic elements between which are assembled the cylindrical volumes of objects and figures. In 1911 form continued to take precedence of color. For at this time, great colorist though he was, Léger deliberately restricted his palette to neutral tones, sometimes of the utmost delicacy (as in *The Smokers*). In 1912, however, he felt his mastery of volume had reached a point where he could safely begin to make use of vivid color. And now he finally broke with that "Montmartre" Cubism which his earlier works, with space reduced to a minimum, had tended to recall, though his predilection for visual experience "in the raw" had always differentiated him from both Braque and Picasso, who refined on their sensations, passing them, as it were, through the sieve of the intellect. Like the Impressionists, Léger aimed at recording in all its eye-filling immediacy the first "impression," untrammelled by any operation of the mind.

We find similar tendencies in Léger's friend Delaunay, whose temperament was strikingly akin to his and who, early in 1909, had, like him, been greatly influenced by Cézanne. Though the 1909 *Self-Portrait* already displays an exceptional mastery of the relations between form and color, it is in the *Saint-Séverin* series

ROBERT DELAUNAY (1885-1941). THE CITY NO. 2, 1910.
MUSÉE D'ART MODERNE, PARIS.

that his originality and creative power are seen at their best. Particularly noteworthy in these pictures is the artist's penetrating study of effects of light. As far back as 1906 Delaunay had noticed how light can modify the shapes of objects. In his views of the church of Saint-Séverin it curves the lines of pillars and breaks up those of the vault and pavement. This disruption of outlines is carried a stage further in subsequent works, notably in his magnificent *Eiffel Towers* of 1910 and 1911. In these light has drastically broken up all the lines and separated

ROBERT DELAUNAY (1885-1941). THE CITY OF PARIS, 1910-1912.
MUSÉE D'ART MODERNE, PARIS.

volumes into isolated groups, viewed in differing perspectives. At the time this led to talk of a "catastrophic art" and Delaunay did not disclaim the epithet; indeed, a little later, he himself described this as his "destructive" period.

In the series of *Cities* this wholesale disintegration of forms by light was carried to its highest pitch. "The spatial dimension is shattered into infinitesimal fragments in all directions" *(Cahiers de Robert Delaunay*, p. 62). But whereas in the "Eiffel Towers" depth still was rendered by means of volumes, it is here conveyed chiefly by color values: a technique Delaunay developed still further early in 1912, in his "Laon" landscapes, where relations of these values suffice *per se* to situate the planes, thus enabling him to dispense with contour lines. All these techniques are synthesized in his big canvas, *City of Paris*, exhibited in the 1912 Salon des Indépendants, which sums up and terminates his "destructive" period, while (in its central part) foreshadowing that method of construction by color alone which was soon to be the keystone of his œuvre.

We are here at a fairly far remove from orthodox Cubism, though the cleavage with traditional perspective, exemplified notably in the "Eiffel Tower" pictures, recalls in a general way the similar break made by Picasso and Braque. Still there are several differences, particularly in the role assigned to light. For Delaunay there is no question of analysing the object so as to get a fuller understanding of it. Far from being the picture's center of interest, it is roughly handled, fragmentated, and partially swallowed up in light, the dominant constructive factor of the composition. Thus, despite many divergencies in their procedures, Léger und Delaunay tended, like the Montmartre painters, toward a common end: the gradual destruction of the unified perspective common to the Renaissance masters, since it cramped their efforts to achieve a completer, more mobile vision of the phenomenal world.

MODERATE TENDENCIES

ASIDE from the sensation it was causing, Cubism could not fail to catch the interest of young painters of the day in quest of a satisfying means of expression. And the sense of a need for a thorough renovation of the whole idea of art was too deep-seated not to lead many of them to feel that the time was ripe for taking serious thought about their aims. It has often, perhaps too often, been said that what several of them saw in the new esthetic was an easy means of getting themselves talked about—and there may well be a grain of truth in this. For, like every epoch-making movement, Cubism had its plagiarists; yet it also pointed the way, in several cases, to sincere and durable vocations. Gifted with originality and talents of unequal quality, some painters, though in no sense pioneers of Cubism, applied themselves to expanding its discoveries or to adapting it, as best they could, to their personal aspirations.

We have not the space to deal with all the "little masters," often considerable artists, who produced what might be styled marginal comments or glosses on the central theme. During the last few years biographies and retrospective exhibitions have done justice—sometimes, perhaps, more than justice— to these lesser men. But there were some belated converts to Cubism who succeeded in giving their art that spice of originality which is often lacking in the work of the immediate disciples of the great pathfinders. Such was the case with Jacques Villon, whose outstanding achievements in this field received the attention they merited only some fifteen years ago.

Though he, too, was led to Cubism by way of a close study of volumes, Villon (pseudonym of Gaston Duchamp) owed nothing, anyhow directly, to Picasso or to Braque. After fifteen years of working as a black-and-white artist for contemporary periodicals he was casting about for a more rewarding manner of expression when his young brother Marcel Duchamp, twelve years his junior, came under the influence of Cubism, as did, not long after, another brother, the sculptor Raymond Duchamp-Villon. Their artistic evolution (as Jacques Villon frankly admits) gave him food for thought. Tired of magazine illustration, dissatisfied alike with the vagueness of Impressionism and the stridencies of Fauvism, he found in Cubism the discipline for which he felt an urgent need. Here at last was a way to *constructing* the picture, architectonically. This trend can be seen as early as 1911, in the portrait of his brother Raymond. The volumes are clearly indicated, full and angular, while a deep chiaroscuro bathing the whole picture surface does not submerge the play of discreetly subdued colors. In *The Dinner Table* of 1912 (exhibited in that year's Salon d'Automne) Villon employed for the first time a system which he was to keep to over a long period: the pyramidal structure advocated by Leonardo. In this system, the lines linking different points in the contours of a volume to an "ideal" point of vision form a pyramid and thus the volume itself assumes a pyramidal form. Sometimes (as in the picture mentioned above) Villon superimposes on these another line, in black, that creates new spatial relations while at the same time stressing the overall rhythm of the composition.

As a result of his first métier, that of illustrator, Villon naturally excelled in drawing, but soon he sought to strike a balance between draftsmanship and color. Though the former still played the leading role in *The Dinner Table* and *Musical Instruments* (Art Institute of Chicago), painted the same year in monochromes of greys and browns, we find his color becoming much intensified from late 1912 on; in, for example, *Man reading a Newspaper*, *Young Girl* (Arensberg Collection), and *Little Girl at the Piano* (Acheson Collection). Here what interests Villon in color is primarily its poetic quality, and this

JACQUES VILLON (1875). LITTLE GIRL AT THE PIANO, 1912.
MRS GEORGE ACHESON COLLECTION, NEW YORK.

has no relation to the local color of the Montmartre painters. Still, while often employing contrasts of pure colors, he did not venture to indulge in clashes of complementaries at their shrillest, as Delaunay was now beginning to do. Villon, in fact, was never such an extremist as Delaunay. Instead of constructing by color Villon began with a considered statement of forms and rhythms and only when this was done did he "clothe" them in color. His aim was not so much to exalt color as to achieve an harmonious whole, since to his thinking the picture should constitute an "object" sufficient to itself. There was in fact nothing revolutionary about Villon's Cubism; it was the result of long, judicious meditation.

For he took a lively interest in discussing the problems raised by the new art and welcomed in his studio at Puteaux, near Paris, Cubists of all persuasions. It was in fact a sort of debating club presided over by Villon and his brothers, at once eclectic and liberal in outlook, and thus contrasting with the stricter disciplines of the Montmartre group. It was the Duchamp brothers who organized, along with Gleizes and Picabia, the famous Salon de la Section d'Or (the idea of naming it after the "Golden Section" came from Villon), in which were represented the most conflicting and heterodox tendencies, ranging from the uncompromising modernism of Marcel Duchamp and Picabia to the neo-classicism of Luc-Albert Moreau and Dunoyer de Segonzac.

Though the two last-named artists may well have seemed somewhat out of place in such an exhibition, it must not be forgotten that Cubism was not confined to the revolutionary-minded vanguard. Villon himself was much less adventurous than his brother Marcel, and some other members of the group had dreams of reconciling Cubism with traditional art. This was the case with two painters of unequal value: Roger de La Fresnaye and André Lhote.

ANDRÉ LHOTE (1885). WOODS AT ARCACHON, 1912.
OWNED BY THE ARTIST.

After infructuous studies at the Académie Julian, La Fresnaye had entered in 1908 the Ranson School of Art where he fell under the spell of two of its promoters, Paul Sérusier and Maurice Denis, whose influence is visible in nearly all his output up to 1910-1911. In his *Shepherd Girl* and especially in *Man drinking and singing* we still find that special atmosphere, at

ROGER DE LA FRESNAYE (1885-1925). LANDSCAPE AT MEULAN, 1911-1912.
COLLECTION OF MR AND MRS RALPH COLIN, NEW YORK.

once hieratic and decorative, which characterizes Nabi art. Even his *Cuirassier* (1910) is not without it, though another influence, that of Cézanne, is now perceptible, notably in the simplification of forms into large volumes, boldly stated and modeled by chiaroscuro. Here color is not so much integrated into volumes as spread upon them and La Fresnaye has obviously been little concerned with the action of light on color. We feel that he still is interested rather in the symbolic and expressive values of the composition than in purely painterly problems.

This will to expression is no less evident in his *Joan of Arc* (1912) which, differing from majority opinion, we do not regard as one of his best canvases. Of greater interest is the series of landscapes La Fresnaye painted during the winter of 1911-1912 at Meulan and La Ferté-sous-Jouarre. In these he employed to good effect the precepts of Cézanne and, though the color orchestration is less rich than the master's, the formal structure is very similar. The composition is built up in successive planes, creating depth, and air circulates freely between them, thanks to variations in the intensity of the light. In such works as *Still Life with Three Handles* (Girardin Collection) and *Married Life,* cubist influence is more in evidence. In these La Fresnaye makes a systematic use of "passages," but instead of disrupting the perspective unity of objects, they serve to modulate transitions, the artist's purpose being to impose classical order and proportion on the composition.

However, *Conquest of the Air*, exhibited at the 1913 Salon d'Automne, and the *Seated Man*, of the following year suggest that La Fresnaye was taking stock of his resources and about to strike out in a new, anti-traditionalist direction. Though color did not play so preponderant a role in his work as in that of Delaunay (whose influence, as pointed out by Apollinaire, is undeniable), there can be no question of an effort to give a new direction to his painting. Indeed there are grounds for

ROGER DE LA FRESNAYE (1885-1925). THE CONQUEST OF THE AIR, 1913.
MUSEUM OF MODERN ART, NEW YORK.

holding that he might have shaped into a great creative artist had not the Great War interrupted his career at its most crucial phase. As it is, however, the neo-classicism of his last years leaves us in doubt as to his true abilities, and it may be suspected that his lifelong ideal was less to open up new fields of art than to adapt a more or less traditional way of seeing to a modernist idiom. This, anyhow, is what his writings indicate, since in them he has no qualms about declaring that even the most advertised artistic innovations really amount to little and merely add something to the edifice built up by previous generations.

In the case of André Lhote this somewhat discouraging conviction assumes the form of an entire philosophy of art. Self-taught, but a highly cultured artist, a theoretician as well a practising painter, he affirms the existence of permanent rules of composition which it is the artist's duty to abide by. "Unaffected by the transformations wrought by genius, by climates, periods, fads, mannerisms and affectations of all descriptions, there exist values which, for want of a better name, I may describe as 'plastic invariants,' a certain quota of which is basic to the life of a work of art" (*Parlons Peinture*, Denoël, Paris, 1933, p. 441). On his view, the artist should begin by scrutinizing nature, and then submit his perceptions to these "invariants." Color must be subordinated to form, and form to a geometric rhythm. "With the result," he continues, "that the responses of the artist's sensibility will not be left in their raw state on the canvas (as was done by the thorough-paced Impressionists), but totally remolded and reorganized according to the rules of traditional composition" (Ibid., p. 80). Obviously pronouncements of this kind tend to reduce Cubism to a set of disciplines perilously near academicism.

GINO SEVERINI (1883). DYNAMIC HIEROGLYPHIC OF THE BAL TABARIN, 1912.
MUSEUM OF MODERN ART, NEW YORK.

CUBISM AND FUTURISM

IT may seem uncalled for to speak of Futurism in a book whose theme is Cubism, given the conflicts between the artists belonging to the two movements, the distance between their centers of activity and, above all, the striking differences in their performances. Yet, on looking closely into the matter, we find that their polemics bore precisely on points that were common to both movements; moreover, that though Futurism was Italian in origin, a good deal of its evolution took place in Paris (where Gino Severini resided) and that, however unlike they superficially appear, we sometimes discover technical affinities in works produced by Cubists and Futurists which prove an underlying kinship. Indeed we may go so far as to say that, allowing for the idiosyncrasies of each of the two movements, they exercised a reciprocal influence on each other, an influence that is well worth studying here, if only for the light it throws on some of the problems discussed in earlier chapters.

Whereas the first Manifesto, signed by F. T. Marinetti and published in the *Figaro* of February 20, 1909, aroused only moderate interest, the futurist painters' Manifesto, signed by Umberto Boccioni, Carlo D. Carrà, Luigi Russolo, Giacomo Balla and Gino Severini, created no little stir when *Comoedia* published the full text in its issue of May 18, 1910 (followed, on June 17, by "Futurist Venice"). Nevertheless, Parisians did not have an opportunity of judging *de visu* the work of the five signatories until their first exhibition took place in February 1912, at the Bernheim-Jeune Gallery, preluding a wave of intense futurist activity in Paris. The Italian artists visited the French capital, gave lectures, published manifestos, held exhibitions, and the many heated controversies between artists or writers these provoked were given wide publicity not only in specialist magazines but in the daily papers.

What attracted most attention was certainly (and naturally enough) the Futurists' insistence on the pictorial value of movement. "Everything moves, all is in a state of flux, of rapid change," runs a passage in their first Manifesto. "An outline is never stationary before our eyes; it is constantly appearing and disappearing. Given the persistence of the image on the retina, objects in movement multiply themselves incessantly and become distorted as they overflow each other like vibrations launched into space and weaving through it at lightning speed." Obviously this notion was at once cinematic and mechanistic.

And aside from some attempts by Severini and Boccioni to integrate energy into the actual *matière* of the painting, most of the Futurists did their best—with varying success—to render movement through a synthesis of the impressions produced by scenes of violent action. Hence the anecdotal nature of their work. Moreover the technique of "lines of force" reduced the expression of dynamism to a system of conventional signs, suggestive in their way, but too greatly simplified to convey the intrinsic vehemence of a sensation of movement. It is to be regretted that these painters failed to understand that any more or less literal visual imitation of such sensations almost inevitably comes up against Zeno's paradox of the arrow in flight. Only *abstract* representation can provide a valid equivalent of movement. Severini seems to have grasped this when from 1912 on he made a point of abstracting the rhythms of the scene before him and imparting to them a more generalized value, universal enough to be capable of expressing other, analogous scenes (for example, Girl Dancing = Sea).

There is no question that, for all its shortcomings, Futurism made a very real contribution to the art of the period; its sincere, if too vociferous, advocacy of an omnipresent "dynamism" could not fail to have profound repercussions and to arouse an interest all the greater for answering to the aspirations of other painters. Still, we should not lend too much credence to the theory that Picasso and Braque were likewise trying to represent movement by a static displacement of lines or the juxtaposition of successive views of the same object. True, an artist of Picasso's caliber cannot have remained indifferent to so vital a problem and Daniel-Henry Kahnweiler states that around

ROGER DE LA FRESNAYE (1885-1925). ARTILLERY (SECOND VERSION), 1912. MR AND MRS SAMUEL A. MARX, CHICAGO.

1910 he even had an idea of "sculptures propelled by clockwork and also pictures that started moving like the targets in shooting galleries when a spring was released" (*Juan Gris*, 1946, p. 176). But this would have meant *real* movement and Picasso never thought seriously of transposing this on to his canvases. The origin of this notion is probably to be found in Gleizes' and Metzinger's *Du Cubisme* (Paris, 1912, p. 36), where there is talk of "moving around an object so as to register its successive aspects which, when combined in a single image, reconstitute it in Time." It is clear that these two painters, anyhow, aspired to express movement by this means. Albert Gleizes, in any case, made a definite assertion to this effect, though frankly admitting that the effect produced could be "illusive."

Futurism seems to have had a more direct influence on some other French artists, among them Roger de La Fresnaye. Though this influence had no permanent effect on his art, its presence can be felt in the second version of *Artillery*, which as it so happens dates to 1912, the very year of the Futurist Exhibition in the Bernheim Gallery. And when we compare the 1912 version with that of 1910, the significance of the change becomes apparent. It is not so much the subject that reveals futurist influences—though possibly inspired by the 1910 Manifesto, it may also be accounted for by La Fresnaye's personal taste for scenes of military life—as the new technique employed by the artist in the second version. In it we find much use of oblique recessive lines and a geometric stylization coming very close to the famous "lines of force" extolled by the Futurists; also a multiplicity of arcs and angles, an interpenetration and a partial disintegration of forms in the lower half of the canvas under the impact of light and movement. True, La Fresnaye imparted to this work an order and clarity very different from the seething chaos of so much futurist art; yet in it we cannot fail to detect reminiscences of earlier works by

JACQUES VILLON (1875). SOLDIERS MARCHING, 1913.
LOUIS CARRÉ COLLECTION, PARIS.

Balla, Russolo and even Severini—and, what is even more significant, the painter seems to be in a quandary as to the direction he now should give his art.

He was not the only one to feel uncertainties of this order. Apart from Léger and Delaunay who were to transpose the problem on to a very different plane, the painters of the "Puteaux Group" (with whom La Fresnaye was in close touch) seem to have given much thought to the new conceptions of rhythm and movement. As we shall see, Marcel Duchamp lit on a wholly original solution, but the works of Jacques Villon show that he, too, was preoccupied with this problem. It was his *Soldiers Marching* (painted in 1913) that above all attracted the attention of contemporary critics and in it the artist's will to express the vital impulse at its most dynamic is manifest. Here a highly abstract arrangement of straight lines and clean-cut angles conveys to perfection the jerky yet strongly rhythmic movement of a regiment on the march. But when we compare *Soldiers Marching* with an authentically futurist composition like Carrà's *Funeral of the Anarchist Galli* we can see that, despite certain resemblances, Villon's art is not to be confused with Futurism. For rendering a more or less similar theme the two artists employ quite different, not to say conflicting techniques, Carrà stressing its figurative, even anecdotal aspects, Villon its plastic qualities. Also, we get an impression that Carrà superimposes his lines of force and interlocking forms on a compositional scheme that is purely classical (resembling the old-style "battle piece"), while Villon makes the rhythms suggested by the scene his starting-point and by way of these approaches the subject proper. Though less conspicuously than here, this preoccupation with rhythm can be sensed in Villon's entire œuvre, notably in his works of the following year such as *The Machine Shop* and *The Equilibrist* (both painted in 1914). In these movement is interpreted by what Villon has described as "the line of the vital urge in all things," this being rendered in the first canvas by the broken rhythms of the angles and in *The Equilibrist* by the sinuous black line in the foreground.

But the problem of representing movement is not the only point on which a comparison between Futurist and Cubist conceptions is rewarding. Their interpretations of what is known as "simultaneity" is no less interesting. For the Futurists the term had a twofold significance: it meant at once a simultaneity of dynamic sensations and a simultaneity of "states of mind." Needless to say, the Cubists were against the second usage—and this is true, despite some ill-considered observations in *Du Cubisme*, of even Gleizes and Metzinger. The romantic, even anthropomorphic subjectivism of all that it implied (did it not assume that even objects were imbued with feelings?) ran counter to their strict concern with factual truth and objectivity. On the other hand, the notion of the simultaneity of dynamic sensations was much more in the cubist spirit, for in practice, it led to the multiplication of viewpoints, since the futurist postulate that the spectator should be posted in the center of the picture could be interpreted on canvas only by the juxtaposition and interpenetration of images that were strictly speaking inconsistent or, anyhow, devoid of the cohesion imposed by normal retinal vision. Indeed, despite the strenuous denials of the Futurists that they owed anything to Cubism, there can be little doubt that their employment of multiple viewpoints would hardly have been feasible had not the Cubists already (in 1910) broken up the unified perspective of classical art. And the futurist interpenetration of forms was no less obviously derivative from the "passages" employed by Picasso and Braque from 1909 on; at a time, that is to say, when the Futurists had not yet dreamt of infringing the rules of academic art or repudiating the opacity of solid objects.

Moreover, this was not their only debt to Cubism. What Severini owed to it is common knowledge, but that Boccioni and Carrà, too, borrowed not a few of its procedures has seldom been remarked on. Yet, besides the use of *papiers collés*, and typographical characters, and their even more frequent use of the characteristic dappled touch of Analytical Cubism, their method of handling volumes quite clearly stems from the Cézannesque phase of Braque and Picasso. Indeed it is not

UMBERTO BOCCIONI (1882-1916).
UNDER THE PERGOLA AT NAPLES, 1914.
GALLERIA D'ARTE MODERNA, MILAN.

going too far to say that some of Boccioni's compositions (*Antigraceful* and *Dynamism of a Woman's Head*, 1912; *Under the Pergola at Naples* and *Man Drinking*, 1914) as well as many of Carrà's works (notably *Rhythms of Objects*, 1911, in the Jesi Collection, and *Simultaneity, Woman and Balcony*, 1912, in the Riccardo Jucker Collection, Milan) are almost more cubist than futurist in appearance.

But we must not be led to what might seem the obvious conclusion: that Futurism was the outcome of a sort of dichotomy of Cubism—the same vision of the world being expressed under two aspects, the one static and the other dynamic. Each of the movements could claim originality, though we may question if the Futurists succeeded in evolving a technique wholly peculiar to themselves; and it well may be that the importance of Futurism in the history of art lies more in its ideas than in its actual achievement. Perhaps it was unable to free itself from the cubist technique of multiple viewpoints, and perhaps that technique was basically unsuited for the expression of movement. Anyhow, to Léger's and Delaunay's thinking, a frankly dynamic vision could be attained only by means of *contrasts*. But it was left to Marcel Duchamp to contribute another solution of the problem.

MARCEL DUCHAMP

AFTER a brief dalliance with the Post-Impressionism of the early 20th century, Marcel Duchamp adopted a mode of painting sometimes Cézannesque *(The Artist's Father)*, sometimes akin to Fauvism *(Dr Dumouchel)*, yet always bearing the imprint of his own personality. It was in 1911 that he came under the influence of Cubism. But instead of (like so many others) concentrating on volumes or even the analysis of objects, he took to exploring certain possibilities of the new art that had so far been little investigated, for example the problem of "transparencies." In *Yvonne and Magdeleine torn in Tatters* and especially in *Portrait of Chess Players* (1911) he seems to be exploiting the facilities provided by Analytical Cubism for simultaneously perceiving objects whose respective positions made it impossible for them to be seen in their entirety under the conditions of normal vision. Thus in the *Chess Players* some of the chessmen can be seen through the cheek of the man on the left, though without detriment to the full rendering of his face. Similarly, by a skillful juggling with light effects so as to displace volumes within the contours of bodies, Duchamp creates an ambiguous type of space in which objects cease to have fixed positions relatively to each other, and seem to interpenetrate; moreover, when we gaze at them for a short time, they seem to come forward or recede, in the manner of figures arranged in reversible perspective. This back-and-forth disposal of planes and volumes already tends to create an impression of movement—though Duchamp does not seem to have had any such intention at the time.

However, in his next works, such as *Sad Young Man in a Train* and *Nude descending a Staircase*, he is clearly concerned with expressing movement in terms of painting, and for this reason many critics have described these works as futurist,

MARCEL DUCHAMP (1887). PORTRAIT OF CHESS PLAYERS, 1911.
PHILADELPHIA MUSEUM OF ART, ARENSBERG COLLECTION.

though he personally has always disclaimed any such influence. And, in point of fact, what Duchamp was trying to do, though it had points in common with the program of the Futurists, was of a quite different order, since he was not endeavoring to

MARCEL DUCHAMP (1887). SAD YOUNG MAN IN A TRAIN, 1911.
PEGGY GUGGENHEIM COLLECTION, VENICE.

MARCEL DUCHAMP (1887). NUDE DESCENDING A STAIRCASE, NO. 2, 1912.
PHILADELPHIA MUSEUM OF ART, ARENSBERG COLLECTION.

represent the movement of a body but the several *static* positions of a body in motion. Thus (as Duchamp himself has explained) the successive profile views of the *Sad Young Man in a Train* do not convey the young man's movement, but imply, by way of static postures of the traveler jolted by the train, the movement of the train itself. In so doing the artist has forestalled the objection raised by Zeno; he does not try to materialize movement but to suggest it by an abstract representation of its consequences. And in this respect he certainly outdid the Futurists, who contented themselves with adding certain conventional signs to academic images. We need only compare *Nude descending a Staircase* (1912) with Russolo's *Plastic Synthesis of a Woman's Movements* (1911) to perceive the radical differences between them. In the center of his canvas Russolo places a woman depicted in a realistic-imitative style; then he goes on to symbolize her changes of position in the manner of a cartoonist, by a series of reiterated curves on either side of her body. Duchamp, on the other hand, abstracts the volumes of the body so effectively that what results is a frankly imaginary creation which, by its very generality, negatives any illusionist individuation. Granted that the *Nude* is not futurist, should it be, then, classified as cubist? On the face of it the presence of simplified volumes, "passages" and so forth suggests an affirmative answer; all the same, some of those who exhibited in Room 41 were not misled by appearances and, just before the 1912 Salon des Indépendants opened, requested Duchamp not to hang this work alongside theirs. For, though owing something to the discoveries of Cubism and Futurism, the artist has boldly "gone one better."

Before long, moreover, Duchamp ceased being satisfied with the traditional means of painting; he was becoming more and more convinced that they were inadequate to capture the mobile, ever-changing aspects of reality. His later works have usually been assumed to be a willful repudiation of the basic media of art. Actually they were, far more, a renovation of them. For the *Ready-mades* were not intended to ridicule art but to prove that a work of art is not necessarily a painted canvas, and it is not its conformity to a conventional mode of presentation but the artist's genius that determines its true artistic value. In virtue of the liberation of his *matière*, Duchamp, from 1913 on, introduced *real* movement into the work of art by means of a wheel rotating on a stool, and subsequently by his *Rotatory Machines* and *Roto-reliefs*. And by these means he demonstrated, successfully, that machine-made objects or disks of colored cardboard could serve as the active principle of works of art no less effectively than colors arranged in a certain order on a canvas—always provided they conveyed the artist's message. Duchamp's inventions and discoveries count for far more than is thought by those who see in them mere dadaist performances. Indeed they are basic to many of the most recent developments of modern art and their power of generating new and striking innovations is far from being exhausted. Is it going too far to say that with these works Duchamp successfully accomplished what the Futurists had in mind, if dimly, but had failed to achieve owing to a paradoxical allegiance to such outworn values as a superstitious faith in the intrinsic "nobility" of certain time-proved media?

FERNAND LÉGER (1881-1955). LANDSCAPE, 1914.
PRIVATE COLLECTION, ROUBAIX.

COLOR AND ABSTRACTION

THE winter of 1912-1913 marked a turning-point in the history of Cubism, for it was then that the art of most of its great creators underwent a profound change, leading to a thorough renovation of the forms and techniques of the earlier period. It was, as we have seen, at the beginning of 1913 that Picasso and, after him, Braque began to practise an intuitive approach and gradually reverted to the use of pure colors. But it was not only under its orthodox form that Cubism was transformed. What took place was, along with a sudden enlargement of its scope, a sort of disruption or, as Apollinaire phrased it, a "quartering" of its structure.

There had been premonitions of the impending change in the 1912 Salon des Indépendants and it was largely with a view to bringing these new tendencies to notice that the "Section d'Or" exhibition was instituted in October of that year. As well as the artists "officially" styled Cubists, there were a number of more independent men, among them Duchamp, Francis Picabia, Henri Valensi and two sculptors, Alexander Archipenko and Raymond Duchamp-Villon, whose productions did not strictly conform to what were then regarded as the basic tenets of Cubism. At the same time, the Salon d'Automne brought to notice several new men such as the Czech Franz Kupka, whose "chromatic fugues" marked a new departure, though their significance had passed almost unnoticed in the mass of canvases exhibited at the Salon des Indépendants. For they constituted an early manifestation of what now is known as abstract or "non-figurative" painting. This tendency had revealed itself, if in varying degrees and without attracting much attention, not only in the too widely dispersed productions of Kupka, but also in those of Wassily Kandinsky, Piet Mondrian and Picabia. Now at last, in the 1913 Salon des Indépendants,

FERNAND LÉGER (1881-1955). THE LAMP, 1913.
COLLECTION OF MR AND MRS LEIGH B. BLOCK, CHICAGO.

FERNAND LÉGER (1881-1955). CONTRASTS OF FORMS, 1913.
PHILADELPHIA MUSEUM OF ART, ARENSBERG COLLECTION.

came the spectacular revelation of the form of art that Guillaume Apollinaire promptly baptized "Orphism" (or "Orphic Cubism"). It gave concrete form to the triumph of color and among its exponents were such very diverse artists as Robert Delaunay, Picabia, Kupka and four Americans: Patrick Bruce, A. B. Frost, Morgan Russell and Stanton Macdonald-Wright.

Color and abstraction were, in fact, the two essential novelties which did so much to enlarge the horizons of Cubism from 1912 onward. True, an excited handling of color had been one of the distinctive characteristics of Fauvism in the first decade of the century, but color was now to acquire a new significance. It was no longer treated as a decorative or emotive element, but as a constructive factor, basic to the expression of space and also to that of dynamism. For this reason it almost always had a non-figurative value, even when associated with formal figurative elements, as in Fernand Léger's compositions.

After a course of self-imposed austerity during the years 1910 and 1911, Léger began little by little to introduce color into his paintings from 1912 on. Timidly used in *The Roofs of Paris* and *Woman in Blue*, color acquires an explosive violence in the works he produced at the beginning of 1913. "When I found I had mastered volume to my satisfaction," he tells us, "I began to give a place to colors. But it was heavy going, and how many canvases I destroyed in those days!... Still, I had a lively feeling for color and was determined to place it in my volumes" (Catalogue F.L., 1956, p. 29). For Léger did not abandon either volumes or contrasts of forms. Unlike Delaunay, who decreed that color should reign supreme, Léger was set on preserving a just balance between what he called in his first lecture at the Wassilieff Academy "those three great pictorial quantities: Line, Form and Color. No work," he went on to say, "can lay claim to pure Classicism, that is to say a permanence enabling it to outlive the period in which it is created, if any one of these quantities is completely sacrificed to the two others." Thus we find Léger systematically contrasting curves with straight lines, flat with modeled surfaces, and primary colors with modulated tones. And since the whole structure of the composition is built up by these contrasts, they create an overall plastic tension of the highest possible potential, generating the dynamism indispensable for an effective representation of the contemporary world. This technique of "multiplicative contrast," as Léger called it, conflicted with the "simultaneous contrast" of colors which, to his thinking, though strengthening the pictorial architecture, did not give color its full efficacy. For, as he pointed out, if two pure colors are juxtaposed they tend to coalesce and cancel each other out, the only way to safeguard their coloristic values being to isolate them as much as possible. Moreover he was convinced that a persistent use of pure colors, however skillfully played off against each other, failed to render the variety needed in renderings of modern life.

This also accounts for the figurative aspects of most of his works. It was, he sometimes said, "the need for variety" that led him to retain them. Actually, however, the reason for this was of a profounder order, for despite the fact that later in life he resorted to "non-objective" methods of expression, he always held that purely abstract art was inapt to convey the restlessness and dynamism of our age. Not that his art was imitative. It was anything but that, and he has stated his views on the subject quite clearly. "The *realistic* value of a work of art is entirely independent of any imitative quality." Realism is, in fact, quite a different thing from imitation, and even an art that studiously refrains from any allusion to the forms of nature —Mondrian's is a case in point, or Delaunay's in *Circular Forms* —may be intensely "realistic" in the true sense of the term. By the same token Léger's art, though figurative, has always an absolute plastic vigor and a wealth of painterly effects. When

FRANCIS PICABIA (1878-1953). UDNIE, 1913.
MUSÉE D'ART MODERNE, PARIS.

he concentrates on the object or on a fragment of an object, this is because he is trying to extract from it a new, more sensitive and truer vision of the world.

Francis Picabia's art, all exuberant imagination, is very different in spirit. Talking, years later, of the dissociation of form from color (the "revelation" of which had come to him

one night on Broadway), Léger frankly admitted that he, personally, could never have thought up this technique. "I've no imagination," he added. Picabia, however, is above all an inventor. Convinced that the outward appearances of the visible have only a relative value, he preferred to reconstruct them as his fancy took him. That is why he was never a Cubist in the full sense of the term. Little is known of Picabia's paintings between his impressionist period and 1912, since some of them he destroyed and many were dispersed in the course of his travels, but it is certain that they were never inspired by orthodox Cubism. Though *Procession at Seville*, which created a sensation at the "Section d'Or" exhibition, reveals an evident concern with volumes, it would seem that Picabia was chiefly preoccupied at the time with relations of forms and colors. Gabrielle Buffet, his first wife, tells us that he then described his esthetic as one of "forms and colors freed from their sensory attributes: a painting based on pure invention and recreating the world of forms according to its own desires, its own imagination" (*L'Oeil*, No. 18, p. 32).

This esthetic is seen to admirable effect in the two large works of 1913, *Udnie* and *Edtaonisl* which thoroughly scandalized the public when exhibited at the Salon d'Automne of that year. Whether the subject is identifiable, as in *Procession at Seville* and *Dances at the Spring*, or transmuted out of recognition as in the two previous canvases, Picabia almost always takes his start from data he has seen or conjured up in his imagination. Thus Gabrielle Buffet tells us that *Udnie* (subtitled "Star Dancer on a Transatlantic Liner") was inspired by the dancer Napierkowska and *Edtaonisl* (subtitled "Clergyman") by a Dominican priest, both of whom he had met on board ship when traveling to New York early in 1913. But even a cursory inspection of these canvases makes it clear that Picabia used his fellow passengers merely as pretexts for compositions having only the slenderest connection with the world of visual appearance. Extremely vivid though rarely contrasted, the colors are not descriptive, but always architectonic. What struck the first spectators of these pictures was, in fact, their chromatic brilliance; hence the tendency to rank Picabia alongside Delaunay, as a practitioner of Orphism. Actually however, the two painters' aims and methods were very different, though, like Kupka (who also passed for an Orphist), they shared a common faith in non-figurative painting.

Actually their conceptions of abstraction were poles apart. For Picabia and Kupka it primarily meant invention, pure pictorial creation without the least concern for realism. The former invented forms as the fancy took him; as one of the pioneers of the Dada movement, he held that his subjective world was quite as real as the objective world. Kupka, however, who owing to his Central European origin came nearer to Kandinsky, held that only the free play of forms and colors enabled the artist to give expression to an inner, purely intellectual and poetic world freed from the trammels of banal physical reality. By means of planes and color harmonies (*Vertical Planes, Amorpha*, 1912) or lines and arabesques (*Solo of a Brown Line*, 1912-1913), he attempts to create "a sort of pictorial geometry of thoughts." Delaunay, on the other hand, saw in abstraction an instrument of realism, a new, more suitable, more telling means of interpreting the "fever and the fret" of modern life and its hectic, syncopated rhythms.

In 1910-1911, like Léger, Delaunay tended to sober down his color. But at the beginning of 1912—partly, we may surmise, under the influence of his wife, the Russian painter Sonia Terk, who practised a distinctively oriental type of Fauvism—he gradually reverted to the use of vivid colors. During the summer and autumn of 1912 he had the notion of making paintings "that, technically, depended solely on color and color contrasts; paintings that unfurled themselves in Time, and were perceived simultaneously, at a single glance" (*Cahiers de R.D.*, p. 81). Indeed, even at the apogee of his cubist period, he had never appreciated the linearism of Picasso's and Braque's art. His friend Léger recalls a visit they made together to Kahnweiler's gallery and Delaunay's exclamation: "Really, these fellows paint with cobwebs!" Now that he had broken up line, any reversion to it would, to his thinking, have been tantamount to a return to the traditional vision from which it stemmed. Something else was needed, and that something else had to be color, "the very basis," as he pointed out, "of the physical means the painter works with."

"The non-objective painting of 1912," he subsequently remarked, "was a direct challenge to the very technique of Cubism. The new technique [by which he meant his own] had no longer any use for chiaroscuro, even perspective, or traditionally rendered volume, that is to say forms first defined by line, then colored, according to the rules laid down by art schools and the tradition stemming from the Renaissance. In *purely coloristic* painting it is color and color alone that, with its breaks, interplays and contrasts, builds up both the formal structure of the picture and its overall rhythms, without the need for any such old-fashioned stand-bys as geometry. Color is *form* and *subject*, sole theme of the picture, and goes its way untrammelled by any sort of 'analysis,' psychological or other" (ibid. p. 67).

This new approach is evident not only in Delaunay's *Windows*, *Disks* and *Circular Forms* but even in his compositions with figures, such as *The Cardiff Team* and *Homage to Blériot* —in all of which form is no longer indicated by drawing but by color. In other words, line ceases to function as a pictorial element and form is defined by the limits of colored surfaces. In the same way space is no longer determined by linear or aerial

ROBERT DELAUNAY (1885-1941). SIMULTANEOUS WINDOWS, 1911.
JEAN CASSOU COLLECTION, PARIS.

perspective, "simultaneous contrasts" of colors sufficing to produce the effect of depth without recourse to chiaroscuro. Though Delaunay, too, tried to justify these contrasts by

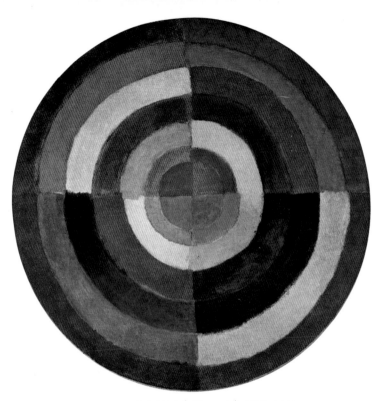

ROBERT DELAUNAY (1885-1941). DISK, 1912.
MR AND MRS BURTON G. TREMAINE, JR., MADISON, CONN.

reference to the theories of Rood and Chevreul, he used them
in a wholly different manner from that of Seurat, who merely
saw in them a means of dispensing with dull or neutral colors.
In Delaunay's compositions they serve a different end; he had
noticed that colors seem to come forward or recede as a direct
consequence of their juxtapositions, area and intensity, and that

these contrasts create new spatial relations. Also they enable the artist to express movement, not like the Futurists by the representation of dynamic subjects or a symbolic use of pictorial signs, but by their mere physical presence. For they cause the colors to "vibrate" in such a way that—again by changes of intensity, by his composition and the areas assigned them—the painter can induce vibrations, slow or fast as he desires. The great novelty of such works as *Disk* and *Circular Forms* came from the use of these spatial and dynamic relations.

ROBERT DELAUNAY (1885-1941). SUN, MOON, 1912-1913.
STEDELIJK MUSEUM, AMSTERDAM.

After the vertical and horizontal contrasts in *Windows*, Delaunay tended, from the end of 1912 on, to dispose his colors in circles, and this enabled him to organize his contrasts more coherently. In *Homage to Blériot* (1914) the circular forms are converted into disks, a procedure that the artist reverted to, and was constantly perfecting, from 1930 until his death. In that picture, as in *The Cardiff Team* (dating to the winter of 1912-1913), Delaunay gives an impression of returning to the anecdotal subject, but here appearances are deceptive. For color, and color alone, is the true subject of the picture in each case, no less than in *Disk* and *Circular Forms*.

Indeed, Delaunay's whole conception of abstraction radically differed from that of such men as Kupka or Kandinsky. "Representation," he declared, "is fundamental to the art of painting, but 'representing' does not mean copying or imitating; it means *creating*" (op. cit., p. 173). Thus allusions to the forms of nature are permissible in so far as these forms have been completely recreated. To his way of thinking, the great thing was not that a painting should be "abstract," but that its technique should be *antidescriptive*, and in his eyes technique was all-important as constituting the decisive element of creation and pointing the way to new discoveries in all the arts. Hence the need to acquire a technical proficiency owing nothing to the past. Delaunay was so strongly convinced of this that he accused the other Cubists of harking back to classical procedures, by way of linearism. "The cause of this state of things, as I see it, is their lack of *métier*" (op. cit., p. 174)—and he went so far as to prophesy the downfall of Cubism.

Piet Mondrian's objection to it was basically of much the same nature. Nonetheless, in 1911 and 1912 he had produced paintings manifestly inspired by the Analytical Cubism of the Montmartre artists (as did many other foreign artists resident in Paris, whom owing to the limited space at our disposal in

ROBERT DELAUNAY (1885-1941). HOMAGE TO BLÉRIOT, 1914.
PRIVATE COLLECTION, PARIS.

the present monograph we cannot deal with individually).
Mondrian, too, insisted on the urgent need for a wholly new
esthetic and, speaking of his early phase, he tells us (vide

Toward the True Vision of Reality in *Plastic Art and Pure Plastic Art*, Wittenborn, New York, 1947, p. 10) that he "gradually became aware that Cubism did not accept the logical consequences of its own discoveries; it was not developing abstraction toward its ultimate goal, the expression of pure reality."

It may, however, be questioned if these objections were justified and if the Cubists really stopped short on the path mapped out by the founders of the movement. More probably Delaunay and Mondrian either failed to notice the new developments of Braque's and Picasso's art in the years 1913 and 1914 or, if they did, to perceive their true significance. For their objections applied only to Analytical Cubism and, had they studied more attentively the Synthetic Cubism that followed, they would have seen that it was as "antidescriptive" as they could have wished, and that it, too, no longer owed anything to classical technique. Moreover, despite differences that it would be idle to deny, and allowing for dissimilarities in the subsequent evolution of members of the group, both orthodox and unorthodox Cubists had arrived, round about 1914, at results which, appearances notwithstanding, both reinforced each other and established the elements of a common language.

It is no easy task to specify these elements, given the fact that not all the artists concerned were equally creative and that even the most creative tended at certain moments to revert to traditional methods they had previously discarded. But if, disregarding these brief digressions, we concentrate on the most significant works of each, it becomes evident that they have a number of features in common which, if not embodying a complete system of representation, make it clear that one was in the making. And it is no less clear that, while some of them failed to implement this program, all the Cubists (except Lhote and La Fresnaye) were, anyhow, resolved to do away with the classical system of the past and replace it with another, better adapted to the requirements of the age. All alike (with the possible exception of Picabia) wished to keep contact with the outside world, and their repudiation of the Renaissance way of seeing did not mean that they dispensed with the idea of "representation," but that all agreed in rejecting conventions that had ended up by garbling the facts of visual experience. Naturally enough it was in the formulation of positive principles that they diverged most widely. Yet, even so, we find that many of their solutions of the problems of contemporary art, though differing in form, were similar in effect—particularly as regards the organization of space.

At first sight, for example, one might say that Braque's and Picasso's *papiers collés* and Delaunay's vividly colored canvases differ *toto coelo*; yet, despite these surface differences, the handling of the spatial dimension in the works of all three artists is much alike. Thus a pasted piece of newspaper upon which a figure has been drawn causes the plane of the figure to move forward in just the same way as an area of red, contrasted with a patch of blue, seems to throw it forward. And similarly Picasso's transparent planes, enabling (for example) a bottle to be seen behind a glass, and those in Duchamp's picture mentioned above, in which we can see chessmen across the cheek of one of the players, are paralleled in Delaunay's *Windows* by the blue and pale green planes that form a luminous screen in front of the Eiffel Tower, without however impairing the integrity of its form. Contradictory though they may seem, there is no doubt that these brilliant innovations ended by providing the point of departure, ill-defined as yet, but rich in possibilities, for a wholly new system of representational signs and spatial relations. Moreover, numerous exhibitions and a steady flow of art books and magazines—not to mention borrowings by poster artists and newspaper cartoonists—had by now done much to make these innovations acceptable to the public at large.

Some art historians have lamented the fact that the World War and its aftermath prevented the formation of a distinctive, fully integrated cubist style. Against this, however, it may be urged that the innovations of Cubism were far too diverse and numerous to be fitted into any cut-and-dried system of forms or codified in a set of formulas. If Cubism ranks as one of the great, not to say the greatest, of the art movements of the first half of the century, and if today its influence, especially on abstract art, is so evident and so vital, the reason is surely that, though departing from the letter, it has loyally kept faith with the spirit of its origin, while the founders of Cubism have, without abandoning its tenets, continually enriched the language they created in the years preceding 1914.

SELECTED BIBLIOGRAPHY
INDEX OF NAMES
LIST OF COLORPLATES
CONTENTS

SELECTED BIBLIOGRAPHY

Source Books and Documentary Material

A. GLEIZES and J. METZINGER, *Du Cubisme*, Eugène Figuière, Paris 1912; English edition, Unwin, London 1913. — André SALMON, *La Jeune Peinture Française*, Albert Messein, Paris 1912. — Guillaume APOLLINAIRE *(Méditation)s Esthétiques. Les Peintres Cubistes*, Eugène Figuière, Paris 1913; reprinted by Pierre Cailler, Geneva 1950; English translation by Lionel Abel, Wittenborn, Schultz, New York 1949.

Art magazines: *Les Soirées de Paris*, Paris, February 1912-June 1913 (ed. A. Billy); 2nd series, November 1913-August 1914 (ed. G. Apollinaire and Jean Cérusse). — *Montjoie!*, Paris, February 1913-March 1914 (ed. R. Canudo). — *Der Sturm*, Berlin, March 1910-July 1914 (ed. H. Walden).

Studies of Cubism

Gustave COQUIOT, *Cubistes, Futuristes, Passéistes*, Ollendorff, Paris 1914; new, revised ed., 1923. — A. J. EDDY, *Cubists and Post-Impressionism*, Chicago 1914; 2nd ed., 1919. — A. SOFFICI, *Cubismo e futurismo*, Florence 1914. — Joàn SACS, *La Pintura Francesa Moderna fins al Cubisme*, La Revista, Barcelona 1917. — Herwarth WALDEN, *Einblick in Kunst : Expressionismus, Futurismus, Kubismus*, Berlin 1917. — Maurice RAYNAL, *Quelques intentions du Cubisme*, L'Effort Moderne, Paris 1919. — Daniel HENRY, *Der Weg zum Kubismus*, Delphin Verlag, Munich 1920; American ed.: Daniel-Henry KAHNWEILER, *The Rise of Cubism*, Wittenborn, Schultz, New York 1949, trans. by Henry Aronson. — Albert GLEIZES, *Du Cubisme et des moyens de le comprendre*, Paris 1920. — Léonce ROSENBERG, *Cubisme et tradition*, L'Effort Moderne, Paris 1920. — P. E. KÜPPERS, *Der Kubismus*, Leipzig 1920. — Gino SEVERINI, *Du Cubisme au Classicisme*, Povolozky, Paris 1921. — "Chez les Cubistes", in *Le Bulletin de la Vie artistique*, November 1, 1924-January 1925. — Albert GLEIZES, *Tradition et Cubisme*, Povolozky, Paris 1927. — Albert GLEIZES, *Kubismus*, Bauhausbücher 13, Albert Langen Verlag, Munich 1928. — Guillaume JANNEAU, *L'Art Cubiste. Théories et réalisations. Etude critique*, Ed. Charles Moreau, Paris 1929. — Catalogue of the exhibition *Les Créateurs du Cubisme*, Gazette des Beaux-Arts, Paris, March-April 1935. — Alfred H. BARR Jr., *Cubism and Abstract Art*, Museum of Modern Art, New York 1936. — Egidio BONFANTE-Juti RAVENNA, *Arte Cubista*, Ed. Ateneo, Venice 1945. — Victor CRASTRE, *La Naissance du Cubisme (Céret 1910)*, Ophrys, n.p., n.d. — Daniel-Henry KAHNWEILER, *Les Années héroïques du cubisme*, Braun, Paris 1950. — Catalogue of the exhibition *Le Cubisme (1907-1914)*, Musée d'Art Moderne, Paris, January-April 1953. — *Le Cubisme*, "Art d'Aujour-d'hui", Boulogne, series 4, No. 3-4, May-June 1953. — Damián Carlos BAYÓN, *Discusión del Cubismo*, in *Ver y Estimar*, Buenos Aires, vol. IX, December 1953. — Christopher GRAY, *Cubist Aesthetic Theories*, Johns Hopkins Press, Baltimore 1953. — Pierre DESCARGUES, *Le Cubisme*, Ed. Aimery Somogy, Paris 1956. — François FOSCA, *Bilan du Cubisme*, La Bibliothèque des Arts, Paris 1956.

Other Works bearing on Cubism

W. H. WRIGHT, *Modern Painting. Its Tendency and Meaning*, John Lane, New York-London 1915. — Franz LANDSBERGER, *Impressionismus und Expressionismus. Eine Einführung in das Wesen der neuen Kunst*, Klinkhardt & Biermann, Leipzig 1919. — Katherine S. DREIER, *Western Art and the New Era*, New York 1923. — OZENFANT and JEANNERET, *La Peinture Moderne*, Crès, Paris 1925. — André WARNOD, *Les Berceaux de la Jeune Peinture, Montmartre-Montparnasse*, Albin Michel, Paris 1925. — Carl EINSTEIN, *Die Kunst des 20. Jahrhunderts*, Propyläen-Kunstgeschichte, vol. XVI, Propyläen-Verlag, Berlin 1926. — Maurice RAYNAL, *Anthologie de la Peinture en France de 1906 à nos jours*, Ed. Montaigne, Paris 1927. — E. JOSEPH, *Dictionnaire biographique des artistes contemporains. 1910-1930*, 3 vols., Paris 1930-1934. — Blaise CENDRARS, *Aujourd'hui*, Grasset, Paris 1931. — Gertrude STEIN, *The Autobiography of Alice B. Toklas*, Harcourt Brace, New York 1933; John Lane, The Bodley Head, London 1933. — *Histoire de l'Art Contemporain*, edited by René Huyghe, L'Amour de l'Art, Paris 1934, chap. VIII and IX. — Raymond ESCHOLIER, *La Peinture Française, XXᵉ siècle*, Floury, Paris 1937. — Gino SEVERINI, *Tutta la vita di un pittore*, Garzanti, Milan 1946. — René HUYGHE, *Les Contemporains*, Ed. Pierre Tisné, Paris 1939, notices by G. Bazin; new ed. 1949. — Maurice VLAMINCK, *Portraits avant décès*, Flammarion, Paris 1943. — Bernard DORIVAL, *Les Etapes de la Peinture Française Contemporaine*, vol. II, Gallimard, Paris 1944. — R. H. WILENSKI, *Modern French Painters*, London-New York, 1940; 2nd ed. 1945; 3rd ed. University Press, Glasgow; Harcourt Brace, New York 1954. — Michel SEUPHOR, *L'Art Abstrait. Ses origines, ses premiers maîtres*, Maeght, Paris 1949. — *Un demi-siècle d'art italien*, Cahiers d'Art, I, Paris 1950. — *History of Modern Painting*, vol. III: *From Picasso to Surrealism*, Skira, Geneva 1950 (chapters on Cubism by Maurice Raynal). — Florent FELS, *L'Art Vivant de 1900 à nos jours*, Pierre Cailler, Geneva 1950. — Pierre FRANCASTEL, *Peinture et Société*, Audin, Lyons 1951. — Paul Ferdinand SCHMIDT, *Geschichte der Modernen Malerei*, W. Kohlhammer Verlag, Stuttgart 1952. — Maurice RAYNAL, *Modern Painting*, Skira, Geneva 1953. — *Dictionnaire de la Peinture Moderne*, F. Hazan, Paris 1954. — Alfred H. BARR Jr., *Masters of Modern Art*, Museum of Modern Art, New York 1954. — Werner HAFTMANN, *Malerei im 20. Jahrhundert*, Prestel-Verlag, Munich 1954. — Werner HAFTMANN, *Malerei im 20. Jahrhundert*, Prestel-Verlag, Munich 1955. — André SALMON, *Souvenirs sans fin*, 2 vols., Gallimard, Paris 1955 and 1956. — Gabrielle BUFFET-PICABIA, *Aires Abstraites*, Pierre Cailler, Geneva 1957. — *Archivi del Futurismo*, De Luca, Rome 1958.

Monographs, Articles, Exhibition Catalogues

Jean PAULHAN, *Braque le patron*, Trois Collines, Geneva-Paris 1946. — *Cahier de Georges Braque. 1917-1947*, Maeght, Paris 1948. — Henry R. HOPE, *Georges Braque*, Museum of Modern Art, New York 1949. — Georges BRAQUE, Dora VALLIER, *La Peinture et Nous*, in *Cahiers d'Art*, Paris, October 1954.

Robert Delaunay, album with 11 pl., catalogue and preface by G. Apollinaire, n.p., n.d. [1913]. — F. GILLES de la TOURETTE, *Robert Delaunay*, Charles Massin, Paris 1950. — *Robert Delaunay*, catalogue of the Delaunay exhibition, Musée d'Art Moderne, Paris, May-September 1957. — *Du Cubisme à l'Art Abstrait. Les Cahiers inédits de Robert Delaunay*, edited by Pierre Francastel, S.E.V.P.E.N., Paris 1957.

View, series V, No. 1, New York 1945 (number devoted to Duchamp). — G. H. HAMILTON, *Duchamp, Duchamp-Villon*, Yale Associates Bulletin, XIII, March 1945. — K. KUH, catalogue of the exhibition *20th Century Art from the Arensberg Collection*, Art Institute, Chicago 1949. — *Jacques Villon, Raymond Duchamp-Villon, Marcel Duchamp*, catalogue of the exhibition *Three Brothers*, Solomon R. Guggenheim Museum, New York, January-February 1957. — Robert LEBEL, *Marcel Duchamp*, Ed. Trianon, Paris 1958.

Albert Gleizes. 50 ans de peinture. Catalogue of the Gleizes exhibition, Chapelle du Lycée Ampère, Lyons, November-December 1947. — Albert GLEIZES, *Souvenirs. Le Cubisme. 1908-1914*, Cahiers Albert Gleizes, I, 1957.

Daniel-Henry KAHNWEILER, *Juan Gris. Sa vie, son œuvre, ses écrits*, Gallimard, Paris 1946; English translation by Douglas Cooper, Curt Valentin, New York 1947; Lund Humphries, London 1947. — *Juan Gris*, Kunstmuseum, Bern, October 1955-January 1956, catalogue by Douglas Cooper. — *Letters of Juan Gris (1913-1927)*, collected by Daniel-Henry Kahnweiler, trans. and edited by Douglas Cooper, privately printed, London 1956. — James Thrall SOBY, *Juan Gris*, Museum of Modern Art, New York 1958.

Anatole JAKOVSKY, *Herbin*, Ed. Abstraction-Création, Paris 1933.

Kupka, catalogue of the Kupka exhibition, Musée d'Art Moderne, Paris, May-July 1958.

E. NEBELTHAU, *Roger de la Fresnaye*, Paul de Montaignac, Paris 1935. — Raymond COGNIAT and Waldemar GEORGE, *Oeuvre complète de Roger de la Fresnaye*, Ed. Rivarol, Paris 1950.

Le Fauconnier, introd. by Jules Romains, Marcel Seheur éd., Paris 1927.
E. Tériade, *Fernand Léger*, Cahiers d'Art, Paris 1928. — Douglas
Cooper, *Fernand Léger et le nouvel espace*, Trois Collines, Geneva 1949. —
Christian Zervos, *Fernand Léger: Œuvres de 1905 à 1952*, Cahiers d'Art,
Paris 1952. —André Verdet, *Fernand Léger, le dynamisme pictural*, Pierre
Cailler, Geneva 1955. — *Fernand Léger*, catalogue of the Léger exhibition,
Musée des Arts Décoratifs, Paris, June-October 1956.

André Lhote, A Study by Anatole Jakovsky, 48 reproductions with
commentaries by the artist, Floury, Paris 1947.

Jean Cassou, *Marcoussis*, Gallimard, Paris 1930. — Alice Halicka,
Hier (Souvenirs), Ed. du Pavois, Paris 1946.

491, René Drouin Ed., Paris, March 4, 1949 (single issue devoted to
Francis Picabia).

Maurice Raynal, *Picasso*, Delphin Verlag, Munich 1921; French ed.,
Crès, Paris 1922. — Wilhelm Uhde, *Picasso et la Tradition Française. Notes
sur la Peinture actuelle*, Ed. des Quatre Chemins, Paris 1928; in English,
New York 1929. — Fernande Olivier, *Picasso et ses amis*, Stock, Paris
1933. — Gertrude Stein, *Picasso*, Scribner's, New York, and Batsford,
London 1938. — Jean Cassou, *Picasso*, Hyperion, Paris 1940; English
translation by Mary Chamot, New York 1940. — Christian Zervos
Catalogue de l'Oeuvre de Picasso, vol. II a and II b, Cahiers d'Art, Paris 1942.
— Ramón Gomez de la Serna, *Completa y veridica historia de Picasso y el
cubismo*, Chiantore, Turin 1945. — Alfred H. Barr Jr., *Picasso: Fifty
Years of his Art*, Museum of Modern Art, New York 1946. — Maurice
Gieure, *Initiation à l'œuvre de Picasso*, Ed. des Deux Mondes, Paris 1951. —
Maurice Raynal, *Picasso*, Skira, Geneva 1953. — Jaime Sabartés, *Icono-
graphie de Picasso*, Pierre Cailler, Geneva 1954. — *Picasso*, catalogue of the
Picasso exhibition, Musée des Arts Décoratifs, Paris, June-October 1955.
— Jaime Sabartés and Wilhelm Boeck, *Pablo Picasso*, Flammarion,
Paris 1955. — José Camón Aznar, *Picasso y el Cubismo*, Espasa-Calpe,
Madrid 1956. — Roland Penrose, *Picasso. His Life and Work*, Victor
Gollancz, London 1958.

George H. Hamilton, *Jacques Villon*, catalogue of the J. Villon-
L. Feininger exhibition, Institute of Contemporary Art, Boston 1949. —
Jacqueline Auberty and Charles Perusseaux, *L'Oeuvre gravé de Jacques
Villon*, Ed. Paul Prouté, Paris 1950. — Jacques Lassaigne, *Jacques Villon*,
Ed. de Beaune, Paris 1950.

Magazines bearing on Cubism

L'Esprit Nouveau, Paris, October 1920-1925, ed. Paul Dermée. —
Le Bulletin de l'Effort Moderne, Paris, January 1924-December 1927 (?),
ed. Léonce Rosenberg. — *Cahiers d'Art*, Paris, January 1926 to the present
day, ed. Christian Zervos.

INDEX OF NAMES

LIST OF COLORPLATES

CONTENTS

THIS VOLUME, THE TWENTY-SEVENTH OF THE COLLECTION "THE TASTE OF OUR TIME", WAS PRODUCED BY THE TECHNICAL STAFF OF EDITIONS D'ART ALBERT SKIRA, FINISHED THE TWELFTH DAY OF APRIL NINETEEN HUNDRED AND FIFTY-NINE.

TEXT AND ILLUSTRATIONS BY THE

COLOR STUDIO

AT IMPRIMERIES RÉUNIES S.A., LAUSANNE

PLATES ENGRAVED BY GUEZELLE ET RENOUARD, PARIS.

PHOTOGRAPHY

Louis Laniepce, Paris (pages 18, 19, 22, 27, 32, 33, 40, 51, 57, 58, 61, 67, 75, 77, 83, 85, 87, 103, 106, 107, 113, 134, 140), Henry B. Beville, Washington (pages 19a, 25, 26, 35, 43, 45, 46, 50, 53, 59, 64, 70, 72, 78, 81, 94, 95, 97, 111, 114, 116, 118, 121, 129, 131, 136, 137, 141, 146), Hans Hinz, Basel (pages 29, 47, 65, 88, 104), Claudio Emmer, Milan (pages 48, 98, 126, 130), Zoltán Wegner, London (page 79), and the photographic services of the Stedelijk Museum, Amsterdam (page 147). Photograph on page 24 obligingly lent by the Editions du Cercle d'Art, Paris.

PRINTED IN SWITZERLAND